Great Meals in Minutes was created by
Rebus, Inc.
and published by Time-Life Books.

Rebus, Inc.

Publisher: Rodney Friedman
Editor: Shirley Tomkievicz
Project Director: Valerie Marchant
Art Director: Ronald Gross
Managing Editor: Fredrica A. Harvey
Assistant Managing Editors: Cynthia Villani,
Ruth A. Peltason
Food Editor: Grace K. Young
Food Stylist: Kim MacArthur
Photographer: Steven Mays
Prop Stylist: Zazel Wilde Loven
Associate Editor: Alexandra Greeley
Production Manager: Peter Sparber
Editorial Assistant: Cathryn Schwing
Editorial Board: Angelica Cannon, Sally
Dorst, Lilyan Glusker, Kim MacArthur, Kay
Noble, Joan Whitman

For information about any Time-Life book,
please write:
Reader Information
Time-Life Books
541 North Fairbanks Court
Chicago, Illinois 60611

Library of Congress Cataloging in Publication Data
Chicken and game hen menus.
    (Great meals in minutes)
    Includes index.
    1. Cookery (Chicken)   2. Cookery (Game)
    3. Menus.
I. Time-Life Books.   II. Series.
TX750.C43   1983   641.6'65   83-4980
ISBN 0-86707-151-0 (lib. bdg.)
ISBN 0-86706-150-2 (retail ed.)

Time-Life Books Inc.
is a wholly owned subsidiary of
Time Incorporated

Founder: Henry R. Luce 1898–1967

Editor-in-Chief: Henry Anatole Grunwald
President: J. Richard Munro
Chairman of the Board: Ralph P. Davidson
Executive Vice President: Clifford J. Grum
Editorial Director: Ralph Graves
Group Vice President, Books: Joan D. Manley

Time-Life Books Inc.

Editor: George Constable
Executive Editor: George Daniels
Director of Design: Louis Klein
Board of Editors: Dale M. Brown, Thomas A.
Lewis, Robert G. Mason, Ellen Phillips,
Peter Pocock, Gerry Schremp, Gerald
Simons, Rosalind Stubenberg, Kit van
Tulleken, Henry Woodhead
Director of Administration: David L. Harrison
Director of Research: Carolyn L. Sackett
Director of Photography: John Conrad Weiser

President: Reginald K. Brack Jr.
Senior Vice President: William Henry
Vice Presidents: George Artandi, Stephen L.
Bair, Robert A. Ellis, Juanita T. James,
Christopher T. Linen, James L. Mercer,
Joanne A. Pello, Paul R. Stewart

Editorial Operations
Design: Anne B. Landry (art coordinator);
James J. Cox (quality control)
Research: Phyllis K. Wise (assistant director),
Louise D. Forstall
Copy Room: Diane Ullius
Production: Celia Beattie, Gordon E. Buck
Correspondent: Miriam Hsia (New York)

SERIES CONSULTANT
Margaret E. Happel is the author of *Ladies
Home Journal Adventures in Cooking*,
*Ladies Home Journal Handbook of Holiday
Cuisine*, and other best-selling cookbooks, as
well as the translator and adapter of Rebecca
Hsu Hiu Min's *Delights of Chinese Cooking*.
A food consultant based in New York City,
she has been director of the food department
of *Good Housekeeping* and editor of
American Home magazine.

WINE CONSULTANT
Tom Maresca combines a full-time career
teaching English literature with writing
about and consuming fine wines. He is now
at work on *The Wine Case Book*, which
explains the techniques of wine tasting.

Cover: Paula Wolfert's sautéed chicken with
tart green grapes, whole garlic, and new potatoes. See page 78.

Great Meals
IN MINUTES

CHICKEN & GAME HEN
MENUS

TIME-LIFE BOOKS, ALEXANDRIA, VIRGINIA

Contents

Meet the Cooks

ANNE BYRD

Born in North Carolina, Anne Byrd grew up watching her grandmother, her parents, and her family cook prepare Southern dishes. She studied at La Varenne in Paris, the Cordon Bleu in London, and the Culinary Institute of America, and she has operated a school in Greensboro, N.C. A founding member of the International Association of Cooking Schools, Anne Byrd has been its president since 1982.

PERLA MEYERS

Author of *From Market to Kitchen Cookbook*, *The Seasonal Kitchen*, and *The Peasant Kitchen*, Perla Meyers has always stressed the use of fresh, in-season foods. She has attended classes at the Ecole Hotelière in Lausanne, the Cordon Bleu in Paris, and the Hotel Sacher in Vienna. She now runs a cooking school in New York City and frequently returns to Europe to visit markets and to work in French, Italian, and Spanish restaurant kitchens.

SHIRLEY SARVIS

San Francisco resident Shirley Sarvis, who began writing about cooking for *Sunset Magazine*, is the author and editor of more than a dozen cookbooks—including her most recent, *Woman's Day Home Cooking Around the World*. She also writes on food and wine for *Gourmet*, *Woman's Day*, *Food & Wine*, *Travel and Leisure*, *Cuisine*, and *Bon Appétit*, among others, and has her own business as a wine and food writer and consultant.

MARY BETH CLARK

Mary Beth Clark is the founder of the Food Consulting Group, a consulting firm for the food, wine, and cookware industries. A Midwesterner who learned to cook professionally in New York, she developed the first Chinese cooking course in America that covered all seven regions of China. At her Manhattan cooking school, she has recently devised new Chinese and American saltless cuisines. She believes that the best cooking relies on freshness and simplicity.

JIM FOBEL

Jim Fobel is the author of *Beautiful Food*, *The Big Book of Fabulous Fun-Filled Celebrations and Holiday Crafts*, and *The Stencil Book*. A former test kitchen director for *Food & Wine* magazine, he writes on food for many national publications. He is the founder of the Picture Pie Company, Stencil-Magic, and The Whole Kit and Kaboodle Company. A graduate of the Otis Art Institute in California, Jim Fobel now lives and works in New York City.

JUDITH OLNEY

Judith Olney, who lives in Durham, North Carolina, is a painter as well as a cook, and in a recent book, *Entertainments*, the look and the taste of each meal get equal artistic billing. Her other books include *The Joy of Chocolate*, *Comforting Food*, and *Summer Food*, and she is an international consultant to Time-Life's *Good Cook* series. A regular contributor to *House and Garden*, *Cuisine*, *Bon Appétit*, and other magazines, Judith Olney has her own television cooking show.

PAULA WOLFERT

Food journalist, cooking instructor, and former chef, Paula Wolfert is also a restaurant consultant. She is the author of *Couscous and Other Good Food from Morocco* and *Mediterranean Cooking*, and she translated *The Secrets of the Great French Restaurants*, by Louisette Bertholle. Her cooking classes focus on Mediterranean—especially French—and Moroccan cuisine. Her most recent book, *The Cooking of Southwest France*, appeared in 1983.

CHRISTOPHER STYLER

Trained as a chef and magazine test kitchen director, Christopher Styler is a cum laude graduate of Johnson and Wales College, the Rhode Island based college internationally known for its culinary division. After serving as chef of The Black Dog Tavern Restaurant on Martha's Vineyard, he went to the test kitchen of *Food & Wine* magazine. From there he joined the staff of *Cuisine* magazine in New York City.

BERT GREENE

The author of *The Store Cookbook*, *Bert Greene's Kitchen Bouquets*, and *Honest American Fare*, Bert Greene likes American cuisine. For 10 years he ran a gourmet take-out shop called The Store on Long Island. He appears regularly as a guest cook on the television show "Hour Magazine," and his weekly food column appears in the *New York Daily News*, the *Los Angeles Times*, and many other papers in between.

Poultry in Minutes

GREAT MEALS FOR FOUR, IN AN HOUR OR LESS

When you want to cook a wonderful meal but do not have much time, chicken is the ideal choice for the main course. You can cook it quickly in at least seven ways: fry, bake, roast, sauté, grill, poach, or steam. You can serve it hot or cold—or at room temperature. It tastes equally delicious when combined with elaborate sauces or the barest few herbs. And it goes with any side dish. Besides all that, chicken is high in protein, rich in iron and the B vitamins, low in calories (if you remove the skin), and economical.

Best of all, everybody likes chicken, the world round. It has been a dietary staple for many centuries. The original breed was a wild jungle fowl of India that villagers and farmers domesticated about 3,000 years ago. Since chickens traveled live, they became the ideal provision on shipboard or overland, and they gradually spread from their native land to every country on earth. Today the menus of France, Italy, China, Japan, India, Africa, the Caribbean, and, of course, the United States are loaded with a marvelous variety of chicken dishes. In the Far East, cooks mince and stir fry it with hot pepper or coat it with spices and broil it. In Mediterranean villages, chicken goes into a shallow pan with shellfish, tomatoes, and rice. In the southern United States it comes deep fried in batter with a ladle of cream gravy. Some of these classic methods have been adapted for this book.

Yet the current generation of cooks is reinventing the repertoire. Chickens have been changing in recent years, especially in the U.S., where most of the birds do not grow up in farmyard coops any more but in computer-controlled feeding factories. Poultry now arrives at our meat counters in an astonishing number of shapes and sizes: boneless cutlets, roasters cut into pieces, stewing fowl, and game hens proliferate, and even quail are available.

At the same time, these mass-produced birds tend to be blander than the old-fashioned barnyard corn scratchers. And American eating and cooking habits have changed, too. Most of us are no longer put off by recipes we once might have thought exotic; in fact, we enjoy trying something new. Moreover, we stock our kitchens with time-saving appliances, special cook pans, choppers, grinders, apple corers, springform pans, food processors, and all

Rock Cornish game hens, opposite, cook to a rich brown in herbs and butter; on the countertop next to the range are several of the fragrant, fresh ingredients that go so well with poultry of any kind: shallots, turnips, chopped parsley, pepper, mushrooms, and olive oil.

manner of other fascinating tools. And we have less time than ever to cook.

On the following pages, 9 of America's most talented cooks present 27 complete menus featuring chicken—or similarly flavored game hens or quail—that can be made in an hour or less. They focus on a new kind of American cuisine that borrows ideas and techniques from around the world but values our native traditions, too. They use fresh produce—no canned vegetables or powdered sauces or other dubious shortcuts. The other ingredients (vinegars, spices, herbs, etc.) are all high quality, yet available for the most part in supermarkets—or, occasionally, in a specialty shop. Each of the menus serves four people and includes side dishes that work perfectly with the poultry.

The color photographs accompanying each meal show exactly how the dishes will look when you take them to the table. The cooks and the test kitchen have planned the meals for good appearance as well as good taste—the vegetables are brilliant and fresh, the color combinations appetizing. The table settings feature bright colors, simple flower arrangements, and attractive, if not necessarily expensive, serving pieces. You can readily adapt your own tableware to these menus in convenient ways that will please your eyes and your guests.

For each menu, the Editors, with advice from the cooks, suggest wines and other beverages—as well as quick, easy desserts—to accompany the meals. And there are suggestions for the best uses for leftovers. On each recipe page, too, you will find a range of other tips—from the fastest way to skin a tomato to the tricks for selecting the freshest produce. All the recipes have been tested meticulously, both for taste and appearance—and to make sure that even a relatively inexperienced cook can do them within the time limit.

BEFORE YOU START

Great Meals in Minutes is designed for efficiency and ease. The books will work best for you when you follow these suggestions:

1. Read the rules (pages 8–10) for selecting and storing chicken, game hens, and quail.

2. Refresh yourself on the few simple cooking techniques on the following pages. They will quickly become second nature and will help you produce professional meals in minutes.

3. Read the menus *before* you shop. Each one opens with a list of all the required ingredients. Check for those

Boning a Chicken Breast

Boning your own chicken breasts saves money and allows you to keep the skin on for the recipes in this volume that call for putting seasoning beneath the skin of boned chicken breasts.

1. Place the whole chicken breast skin side down—allow about one and a half pounds per serving. Slit the white membrane that covers the breastbone. **2.** Grasp the breast in both hands and bend it away from you to break the breastbone and piece of cartilage. Pull up on the dark breastbone and remove it. **3.** Turn the breast around. Push with your thumbs on either side of the white cartilage in the center of the breast, and then pull it off. **4.** Using a knife, cut under the ribs on either side of the breast and remove them. Always hold the blade of the knife next to the bones so you do not pierce the flesh. **5.** Pull up on the wishbone and remove it by carefully running the top of your knife around and under it. **6.** Turn the breast. Hold the end of the membrane that runs up the middle, and scrape away the meat. **7.** The two small fillets on each side of the breast (indicated by dotted lines) have tough tendons that should be removed. Grasp one end of the tendon and pull it toward you, scraping it away from the flesh with your boning knife. Each breast weighing about one half pound boned and skinned is suitable for one serving.

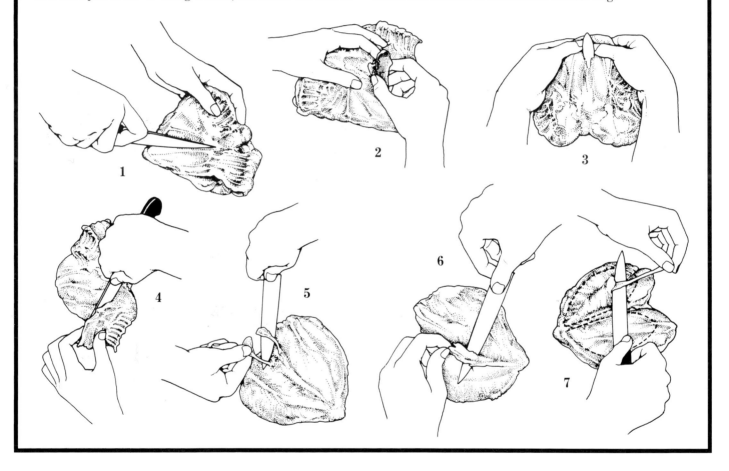

few you need to buy; most items will already be on your pantry shelf.

4. Check the equipment lists on pages 16–17. A good, sharp knife—or knives—and pots and pans of the right shape and material are essential for making great meals in minutes. This may be the time to look critically at what you own and to plan to pick up a few things. The right equipment can turn cooking from a chore into a creative experience.

5. Get out everything you need before you start to cook: the lists at the beginning of each menu tell just what is required. To save steps, keep your ingredients close at hand and always put them in the same place so you can reach for them instinctively.

6. Take chicken and dairy products from the refrigerator early enough for them to come to room temperature so as to cut cooking time.

7. Follow the step-by-step game plan with each menu. That way, you can be sure of having the entire meal ready to serve at the right moment.

SELECTING THE RIGHT CHICKEN

You can find fresh chickens in any supermarket, anywhere, thanks to modern shipping and refrigeration methods. Many birds reach the butcher or supermarket 24 hours after they have been killed. And chickens kept in a properly cooled display case stay fresh for up to seven days. If possible, avoid chickens that have been frozen and then defrosted: and if you are not sure whether a bird has been frozen, inquire. Defrosted chicken spoils quickly, nor is a thawed chicken ever quite as flavorful as a fresh one.

All supermarket poultry comes from mass-producers, who cage-raise birds by the tens of thousands. If you live near a farm and can buy fresh-killed, free-range chickens—birds that scratched around outside for their food— you know that these birds have a richer flavor than the commercial ones. Nevertheless, the advantages of the standard supermarket chicken—availability, ease of preparation, cleanliness, and low price—more than make up for its loss of flavor as compared with chickens raised on old-fashioned farms. And, as the recipes in this book are intended to show, there are many delicious ways to enhance the mild flavor of modern poultry—with herbs and seasonings, with uncomplicated sauces, and with compatible side dishes.

Whatever your source, you must pick out the right bird for your chosen menu. Markets sell chickens under different names and according to size and age. For most of the recipes in this volume, broilers or broiler-fryers are best. They weigh from one and a half to three pounds and are between seven and eight weeks old. Slightly larger chickens, called fryers, weigh up to four pounds and are just as tender and moist, but they take a little more time to cook. *For one serving, allow three fourths of a pound raw chicken with bone and skin, but one third to one half of a pound when the chicken is boned and skinned.*

Despite their names, all these smaller birds can be roasted, sautéed, steamed, or poached—as well as broiled and fried. The bigger and older chickens, known as roasters, though usually better flavored, need more than an hour to cook and therefore are not dealt with in this book.

Whether you are buying whole birds or packages of parts, look for broiler-fryers with the Grade A inspection stamp of the U.S. Department of Agriculture. Grade A chickens conform to a set of standards covering the shape, the amount of fat in relation to the amount of meat, and the general condition of the skin. A Grade A stamp means that the chicken is meaty, that it was healthy and free of defects when slaughtered, and that both the chicken and the plant where it was processed were inspected.

Do not stop inspecting with the grading stamp. Smell the chicken or the package. A fresh chicken has no odor, or almost none. A fresh-killed broiler-fryer will have a pliable breastbone and a moist, but not sticky, skin.

One other point about freshness: you may have heard that skin color is a good indicator, that a really fresh, well-raised chicken will be very yellow, or very white. In fact, skin color comes from the kind of feed the chicken ate and is not an indication of freshness. It merely reflects regional consumer preferences, which the growers try to accommodate. Most chickens sold on the West coast have a white skin; those sold in the North and Northeast tend to be pale yellow. (You should take note, however, if the color of a bird's skin is purplish—this does indicate that the bird is past its prime.)

Game Hens and Quail
The Rock Cornish game hen, a cross between an English

Testing for Doneness: Why and How

A properly cooked chicken breast will be white through, with no sheen as you slice through it. Dark meat should slice easily and exhibit no tinge of pink.

Chicken is not a meat to serve rare. Not only would most people find it unappetizing, but undercooked poultry is not wholesome. Even high quality chicken meat may carry bacteria, which fortunately are destroyed in the normal cooking process. On the other hand, overcooking a chicken leaves it dry and tasteless. Every recipe in this volume of course specifies cooking time, but since kitchen ranges (and other factors) may vary, you should know the three methods of testing for doneness. Begin to test a minute or so before the specified time is up. Remember that breast meat cooks faster than dark and that unless you are serving chicken immediately, it will continue to cook in its own heat. Allow for that extra three to five minutes if you plan to let the chicken sit.

1. *The instant-reading meat thermometer.* This lightweight little tool is handier and better than the old-style roasting thermometer, which must sit in place while the meat cooks. Insert the tip into the thickest part of the meat. Be sure the tip does not touch bone, which gives a higher reading.
   Poultry is done at 180–185 degrees.

2. *Touch.* Test lightly with thumb and index finger. Cooked chicken has a springy feel, slightly resistant to indentations. You need experience to recognize the signs, so practice with the aid of a thermometer. When cooking a whole chicken, try moving the drumstick. It should feel loose, almost detachable— but do not allow the meat to reach the falling-off stage.

3. *Piercing.* This should be a last resort, since it spoils the appearance, as well as allows juices to escape. Still, if you have no meat thermometer and cannot calm your doubts by method 2 above, pierce the thickest part of the breast or thigh with a fork. Juices should run clear.

---

chicken from Cornwall and the American White Plymouth Rock, is all white meat. The flavor is a little blander than a supermarket chicken and thus requires a touch more in seasonings or sauces. The smallest of all true chickens, the Cornish hen should weigh less than one pound, which makes one hen about right for a single serving. Poultry growers have recently tended to market older game hens, and you may have trouble finding the convenient one-pound size. (The game hen recipes in this book work equally well with the larger game hens.)

The quail, a tiny relative of the pheasant and common in the South, weighs only five to six ounces and has almost no body fat. Count on two quail per serving—and reserve them for special occasions.

Most supermarkets carry fresh or frozen game hens regularly, and the rules for selecting them are the same as for chicken. Many markets also stock frozen, or even fresh, quail.

Storing Poultry

Poultry tastes best when cooked and eaten as soon as possible, ideally within 24 hours after you buy it. (Make sure you use it within three days.) As soon as you get home, take the bird—whether it is a chicken, hen, or quail—out of the market package, put it on a plate or platter, rewrap it loosely in waxed paper so that air can circulate, and refrigerate it. An airtight wrap makes for quicker spoilage. Wash the giblets (neck, heart, gizzard, and liver) and freeze them, for they are very perishable. None of the recipes in this book calls for giblets, but you can use the neck and gizzard in stock (see page 11).

When freezing a bird, wrap it tightly in heavy foil or freezer wrap, forcing out as much air as possible. A loose wrap permits freezer burn, which dries out the meat and spoils its appearance. Always label the package with the date. (Keep a roll of masking tape and a ball-point pen handy for making quick kitchen labels of all kinds.) Poultry kept at zero degrees can be safely frozen for six months. However, the freezing compartments of most refrigerators do not get cold enough for such long-term storage. Two weeks or so is the sensible maximum if you want to preserve the flavor. Chicken kept longer than a month in the freezing compartment should probably go into the stockpot.

Thawing

Thaw poultry slowly: quick thawing tends to reduce the flavor. The best method is to let the bird thaw in the regular food compartment of your refrigerator. This takes about two hours per pound (a three-pound chicken needs a long afternoon to thaw) but it helps the flavor and reduces the chance of bacteria forming as the temperature rises. Do not remove the freezer wrap until the bird is completely defrosted. To decrease cooking time, take the chicken from the refrigerator and let it come to room temperature before cooking. This should take no more than two hours—one hour if the room is very warm.

If you do not have the time for this preferred method, thaw the wrapped bird at room temperature, allowing about one hour per pound. In an emergency, you can unwrap poultry and thaw it fast in a bowl of cold water. To speed things along, pull the legs and wings away from the body as soon as you can pry them loose. A three-pound

chicken should thaw in about an hour this way. Never defrost a frozen chicken in hot water—however great the temptation may be. The surface of the meat will begin to cook and then will turn dry and tasteless in the recipe.

Be sure to wipe a defrosted bird inside and out before cooking.

COOKING TECHNIQUES

Pounding

Pounding a boned chicken breast flattens it so that it will cook evenly and quickly. Several recipes in this volume call for this simple technique. Place a boned chicken breast between pieces of plastic wrap. Pound with the flat side of a heavy cleaver or a meat pounder, moving from the center out to the edges so it is of even thickness.

Sautéing

Sautéing is a form of quick frying, with no lid on the pan. In French, *sauter* means "to jump," which is what vegetables or small pieces of food do when you shake the sauté pan. Sautéing is the cooking method used for chicken and game hens in a number of the menus that follow. The purpose is to lightly brown the chicken pieces—or whole game hens—and seal in the juices before further cooking. This technique has three critical elements: the right pan, heated to the proper temperature, and a dry chicken.

The Sauté pan: A proper sauté pan is 10 to 12 inches in diameter and has 2- to 3-inch straight sides that allow you to turn the chicken pieces while keeping the fat from spattering. It has a heavy bottom that slides easily over a burner.

The best material (and the most expensive) for a sauté pan is tin-lined copper because it is a superior heat conductor. Stainless steel with a layer of aluminum or copper on the bottom is also very efficient. (Stainless steel alone is a poor conductor.) Heavy-gauge aluminum works well but will discolor acid food such as tomatoes. Therefore, you should not use aluminum if the food is to be cooked for more than twenty minutes after the initial browning. Another option is to select a heavy-duty sauté pan made of strong, heat-conductive aluminum alloys. This type of professional cookware is smooth and stick-resistant.

The ultimate test of a good sauté pan is whether or not it heats evenly: hot spots will burn the food rather than brown it. A heavy sauté pan that does not heat evenly can be saved. Rub the pan with a generous amount of vegetable oil. Then place a half inch of salt in the pan and heat it slowly over low heat, about 10 to 15 minutes, until very hot. Empty salt, do not wash the pan, and rub it with vegetable oil again.

Select a sauté pan large enough to hold the chicken pieces without crowding. The heat of the fat, and air spaces around and between the pieces, allow browning. Crowding results in steaming—a technique that lets the juices out rather than sealing them in. If your sauté pan is too small to prevent crowding, separate the chicken into two batches, or use two pans at once.

You will find sauté pans for sale without lids, but be sure you buy one with a tight-fitting cover. Many recipes call for sautéing first, then lowering the heat and cooking the chicken, covered, for an additional 10 to 20 minutes. Make sure the handle is long and comfortable to hold.

When you have finished sautéing, never immerse the hot pan in cold water—this will warp the metal. Let the pan cool slightly, then add water, and let it sit until you are ready to wash it.

Use a wooden spatula or tongs to keep the chicken moving in the pan as you shake it over the burner. If the meat sticks—as it occasionally will—a metal turner will loosen it best. Turn the pieces so that all surfaces come into contact with the hot oil and none of them sticks. Do not use a fork—piercing the chicken will cause the juices to run out and will toughen the meat.

The fat: A combination of half butter and half vegetable or peanut oil is perfect for most sautéing: it heats to high temperatures without burning and allows you to have a rich butter flavor at the same time. Always use unsalted butter for cooking: it tastes better and will not add unwanted salt to your recipe. Butter alone makes a wonderful-tasting sauté; but butter, whether salted or unsalted, burns at a high temperature. If you prefer an all-butter flavor, clarify the butter before you begin. This means removing the milky residue, which is the part that

---

Making Chicken Stock

Although canned chicken broth or stock is all right for emergencies, homemade chicken stock has a rich flavor that is hard to match. Moreover, the commercial broths—particularly the canned ones—are likely to be over salted.

To make your own broth, save chicken parts as they accumulate and put them in a bag in the freezer; then have a rainy-day stock-making session using one of the recipes below. The skin from a yellow onion will add color; the optional veal bone will add extra flavor and richness to the stock.

3 pounds bony chicken parts, such as wings, back, and neck
1 veal knuckle (optional)
3 quarts cold water
1 yellow unpeeled onion, stuck with 2 cloves
2 stalks celery with leaves, cut in 2
12 crushed peppercorns
2 carrots, scraped and cut into 2-inch lengths
4 sprigs parsley
1 bay leaf
1 tablespoon fresh thyme, or 1 teaspoon dried
Salt (optional)

1. Wash chicken parts and veal knuckle (if you are using it) and drain. Place in large soup kettle or stockpot (any big pot) with the remaining ingredients—except salt. Cover pot and bring to a boil over moderate heat.

2. Lower heat and simmer broth, partly covered, 2 to 3 hours. Skim foam and scum from top of broth several times. Add salt to taste after broth has cooked 1 hour.

3. Strain broth through fine sieve placed over large bowl. Discard chicken pieces, vegetables, and seasonings. Let broth cool uncovered (this will speed cooling process). When completely cool, refrigerate. Fat will rise and congeal conveniently at top. You may skim it off and discard it or leave it as protective covering for broth.
Yield: About 10 cups.

The flavor of chicken stock comes from the bones (as well as the seasonings and vegetables) rather than the meat. The longer you cook the bones, the better the stock. If you would like to poach a whole chicken and want to make a good, strong stock at the same time, this highly economical recipe will accomplish both aims at once.

Strong Chicken Stock

10 cups homemade chicken broth (yield of recipe above)
1 whole broiler or fryer (about 3 pounds)
1 bay leaf
1 stalk celery
1 carrot, scraped
1 yellow onion, unpeeled

1. Add liquid, vegetables, and seasonings to kettle large enough to hold them and chicken. Bring to a boil over moderate heat.

2. Add chicken, breast up, and allow liquid to return to a simmer. Reduce heat and poach chicken with lid slightly ajar.

3. After 40 minutes, test for doneness. Insert long-handled spoon into chicken cavity and remove chicken from broth to platter.

4. When chicken is cool enough to handle, but still warm, debone it, reserving meat for salads or sandwiches but returning skin and bones to cooking pot. Continue to simmer, uncovered, until stock has reduced by half. Proceed as in step 3, above.

Added Touch: If you have time and want a particularly rich-looking stock, put the chicken bones in a shallow baking pan and brown them under the broiler for 10 minutes before you add them to the stock.

Stock freezes well and will keep for three months in the freezer. Use small containers for convenience and freeze in pre-measured amounts: a cup, or half a cup. Or pour the cooled stock into ice cube trays, then remove the frozen cubes and store in a plastic bag. You can drop these frozen cubes directly into your saucepan.

scorches. To clarify, heat the butter in a small saucepan over medium heat and, using a cooking spoon, skim off the foam as it rises to the top, and discard it. Keep skimming until no more foam appears. Pour off the remaining oil, making sure to leave the milky residue at the bottom of the pan. The oil is clarified butter; use this for sautés. Some sautéing recipes call for olive oil, which imparts a delicious and distinctive flavor of its own and is less sensitive than butter to high heat. Nevertheless, even the finest olive oil has some residue of fruit pulp, which will scorch in high heat. Watch carefully when you sauté in olive oil; discard any scorched oil and start with fresh if necessary.

To sauté properly, heat the sauté fat until it is hot but not smoking. When you see small bubbles on top of the fat, it is almost hot enough to smoke. In that case, lower the heat. When using butter and oil together, add the butter to the hot oil. After the foam from the melting butter subsides, you are ready to sauté the chicken. If the temperature is just right, the food will sizzle when you put it in.

The chicken: Just before sautéing, wipe the chicken pieces with paper towel to be certain they are completely dry. Wet chicken will spatter in the fat and will not begin to brown until the water evaporates, by which time some of the juices will have been lost. Put the chicken in the sauté pan with its skin side down, brown it, then turn it.

Searing

Searing is almost the same as sautéing, but you need slightly hotter fat, and when you sear, you allow the meat to brown without shaking or stirring the pan. Heat the fat until it is very hot (at least 350 degrees), then brown the chicken over high heat for a minute or two on each side. A metal turner is essential, for the chicken will tend to stick. Wait to turn it until it is very brown. Mary Beth Clark's recipes for stuffed chicken breasts (see pages 46–55) call for searing the edges of each breast as well as the top and bottom. You can do this by holding the breasts on end with tongs.

Deep-Fat Frying

People often say pan fry when they mean sauté. But frying calls for more fat than does sautéing; and fried chicken is usually coated with batter and then immersed in hot fat.

The best way to fry is to heat the fat slowly to between 360 and 375 degrees in a deep iron skillet or other heavy high-sided pan. Use a deep-fat thermometer or test the temperature by frying a small cube of bread—which should brown in less than a minute when the fat is hot enough. The temperature is important: underheating will cause the food to absorb oil, and overheating will scorch the chicken.

Use vegetable or peanut oil—never butter alone, or a mostly butter mixture. But for a traditional Southern fried chicken, try Anne Byrd's recipe (see page 21). She uses a combination of lard (rendered pork fat) and butter.

Whatever fat you use, slide the chicken pieces gently into the pan using a pair of tongs. Hot fat will spatter dangerously if you drop food into it.

Deglazing

To deglaze a pan in which chicken has been cooked means simply to remove the chicken and to pour off any fat in excess of one or two tablespoons and then, with the pan over medium heat on top of the range, to pour liquid into it—stock, water, or wine—and reduce the liquid. As this liquid reduces, you scrape the sides and bottom of the pan with a long-handled spoon (wooden if possible) to pick up any tiny bits of brown meat, congealed juices, herbs, and any other good things clinging to the pan. The resulting liquid, without any thickening agent added, is basic to many of the sauces in this book; indeed, deglazing is a technique basic to most gravy and sauce making. (An additional benefit: a deglazed pan is much easier to wash.)

Degreasing

In degreasing a pan you remove the accumulated fat from the liquid in which the chicken cooks. Let the liquid settle for a few minutes after cooking, and the fat will rise to the surface. Skim it off with a long-handled spoon. You can then blot the top of the liquid with paper towels to remove the remaining globules. If your chicken is still roasting and you wish to degrease, just tilt the pan juices to a corner and skim off the fat. The easiest method—but the one requiring time—is to chill the liquid and then scrape the congealed fat off the top.

Poaching

You poach a chicken exactly as you would poach an egg—in very hot liquid, in a shallow pan, on top of the stove. For chicken, you can use water or, better still, chicken stock or a combination of chicken stock and white wine. Bring the liquid to the simmering point and add the chicken (usually a boneless breast). Be prepared to watch carefully and to lower the heat if the water begins to boil, reducing the water to a bare simmer. Boiling toughens the meat and dries it out. Poaching is an ideal summer cooking method since it uses so little heat, and poached chicken is good cold. Since poached chicken will be pale, bright garnishes, such as the homemade tomato mayonnaise on page 91, make it look very tempting.

Steaming

A fast and nutritious way to cook vegetables, steaming is also an excellent method for cooking chicken. Bring water, or a combination of stock and wine, to a boil in a steamer (see diagram page 17). Place the chicken in the steaming-basket or rack over the liquid, and cover—periodically checking the water level. Keeping the food above the liquid preserves vitamins and minerals. Like poached chicken, steamed chicken is mild tasting and pale, as well as low in calories. It takes well to garnishing and saucing.

Roasting and Baking

A roasted chicken cooks in the oven, whole and uncovered. To roast, season the chicken inside and out, and rub it with softened butter. Baste it several times during roasting with the drippings that collect in the pan. Shirley Sarvis recommends roasting a small broiler-fryer for 15 minutes breast side down, and then turning the chicken on its back

Disjointing a Chicken

Disjointing a whole chicken takes only minutes and produces 8 or 10 portions (4 with breast meat) that you can quickly sauté or fry. You save money by doing your own disjointing, because whole chickens are fresher and cheaper per pound than chicken parts, and you have the added bonus of backbone, neck, and giblets for your chicken stock. The only tricks are to find all the joints—thigh, leg, and wing—and to cut through cleanly at those points. You need a sharp knife, and poultry shears are a great help too.

1. Set the bird on its back and pull one leg away from the body. Cut through parallel to the backbone at the joint. Then cut the thigh and leg apart at the joint. Repeat with the other leg. **2.** Pull the wing away and cut through, starting inward diagonally, at the shoulder joint; then slice toward the rear. Repeat with the other wing. **3.** Using the knife or the poultry shears, cut through the ribs along either side of the backbone. **4.** Open up the body and cut between the breast and the backbone. Place the breast skin side down and push down with your hands to flatten it. **5.** Cut the breast in half lengthwise—and then into quarters if you want 10 serving pieces.

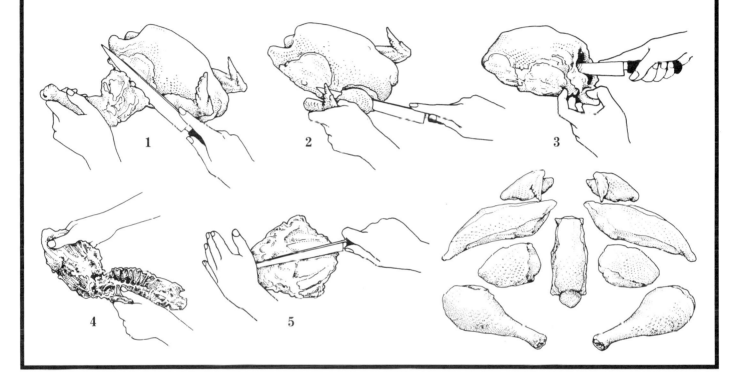

and cooking for another 35 minutes (see pages 40–41).

To bake a chicken, you disjoint it and put it in the oven in a covered casserole—usually with a sauce. Baking is best for chicken quarters or smaller pieces. Some recipes call for sautéing the chicken before transferring it to the baking dish, where it cooks in a cream or wine sauce.

Broiling and Grilling

These are two relatively fast ways to cook a bird. If you are using a whole chicken or game hen, you should cut out the backbone and flatten the bird first (see diagram page 74). Otherwise it would never cook through. Whether broiling or grilling, brush the bird with melted fat, a sauce, or a marinade before you cook it. This adds flavor and keeps the poultry moist under the high heat. Jim Fobel (see page 59) and Judith Olney (see page 74) both use this method.

In broiling, the chicken or hen cooks directly under the source of the heat. To ensure that the flesh is done before the skin burns, move the broiling rack five to six inches from the heat source.

In grilling, the bird cooks directly over the heat source—frequently a bed of charcoal. Set the grill far enough away from the heat so that the skin does not burn. With a good bed of coals, the right grill height might be four inches, but you must watch carefully for a few minutes to gauge the proper distance. Once it is browned on all sides, cover the chicken with the grill cover (or a tent of aluminum foil) while it is cooking.

Flambéing

Flambéing makes a dramatic point at any meal. It requires igniting an already-warm liqueur in the pan juices of the chicken. Brandy or a liqueur should not be close to a boiling point when you pour it over the chicken. Be sure to remove your pan from the heat, then avert your face and ignite the brandy with a lighted match. A quiet flame will burn for a few seconds. Shake the pan a bit to baste the chicken and seal in moisture. Anne Byrd uses this method with her chicken with mushrooms (see page 23). Allow about an ounce of liqueur per person when flambéing. The taste remains, but the alcohol burns off—and you have enjoyed a moment of showmanship.

Pantry (for this volume)

A well-stocked, properly organized pantry is a time-saver for anyone who wants to prepare great meals in the shortest possible time. Location is the critical factor for staple storage. Whether your pantry consists of a small refrigerator and two or three shelves over the sink or a large freezer, refrigerator, and whole room just off the kitchen, you must protect staples from heat and light.

In maintaining or restocking your pantry, follow these rules:

1. Store staples by kind and date. Canned goods need a separate shelf, or a separate spot on the shelf. Put the oldest cans in front, so that you need not examine each one as you pull it out. Keep track of refrigerated and frozen staples by jotting the date on the package or writing it on a bit of masking tape.

2. Store flour, sugar, and other dry ingredients in cannisters or jars with tight lids, where they will last for months. Glass or clear plastic allow you to see at a glance how much remains.

3. Keep a running grocery list near where you cook so that when a staple such as olive oil, sugar, or flour is half gone, you will be sure to stock up.

ON THE SHELF:

Baking powder

Baking soda

Chicken stock

Canned stock, or broth, is adequate for most recipes and convenient to have on hand; but you may prefer to make your own (see page 11).

Cornstarch

Flour

All purpose (ground for any use from cakes to bread), bleached or unbleached.

Herbs and spices

Fresh herbs are always best; the flavor is much better than in dried herbs. Many fresh herbs are now available at produce markets. If you like, you can grow basil, chervil, oregano, sage, and—depending on climate—several other herbs in a small garden outdoors or on a sunny windowsill. Fresh herbs should be used immediately. The following herbs and spices, however, are perfectly acceptable in their dried or packaged form— but buy in small amounts and use as quickly as possible. In measuring herbs, three parts of fresh herbs will equal one part dried. *Note:* Dried chives and parsley should not be on your shelf, since they have little or no flavor. But freeze-dried chives are acceptable.

allspice (whole)
anise
basil
bay leaves
chervil
cinnamon (ground)
cloves (whole)
coriander
cumin
fennel
marjoram
mustard (dry)
nutmeg (whole)
oregano
paprika
pepper

black, whole peppercorns
These are ripe peppercorns dried in their black skins. Grind for each use with a pepper mill.

green, whole peppercorns
Peppercorns picked and packed in jars before ripening. Taste milder than the dried black peppercorn variety and are used whole, rather than cracked or ground. For best flavor, buy brands packed in brine rather than in vinegar.

red pepper flakes
Also called crushed red pepper.

red chili pepper, dried

Cayenne pepper

ground red chili pepper

white, whole peppercorns
These are like the black variety but are dried without the dark skin. Use them in pale sauces when black pepper specks would spoil the appearance.

rosemary
sage
salt

Use coarse—also known as kosher—salt because of its superior flavor and coarse texture. It is pure salt with no additives. Kosher salt and sea salt taste saltier than table salt. When the recipe calls for kosher or sea salt, you can substitute in the following portions: three quarters teaspoon kosher or sea salt equals one teaspoon table salt.

savory
tarragon
thyme

Oils

corn, peanut, or vegetable
Because these neutral oils add little or no taste to the food and have high smoking points, use them for sautéing.

olive oil
American olives are mostly canned for eating, not pressed for oil. The best oils are imported. Sample French, Greek, Spanish, and Italian oils (Luccan oil, from the Tuscan region, is sure to be in your supermarket) until you find the taste you like best. Each has its own flavor. Buy only virgin or first-pressing oil; the oil from the second pressing is full of fruit pulp that burns at high heat.

Good olive oils may vary in color from green to golden yellow. The pale and less expensive oils are fine for cooking.

sesame oil (Chinese and Japanese)
Used as a seasoning in Oriental cooking and sold in the Oriental section of most supermarkets. Keeps indefinitely when refrigerated. (Middle Eastern sesame oil is useful for cooking but quite different in character and no substitute for Chinese and Japanese sesame oil. You will not need the Middle Eastern oil for any recipe in this volume.)

sunflower oil
Light, mild, and good for cooking.

walnut oil
Strong, nutty flavor. Because it is expensive and does not keep well, buy it in small quantities: Specialty stores and some supermarkets stock it.
Storage note for oils: If you keep oils in a pantry away from light, they should last for three months, unless room temperature is always high. If oil has gone rancid, you can detect it by the stale, almost dirty smell. Throw it out at once—there is no way of rescuing it. If you notice that your oils tend to go bad, keep them in the refrigerator. They will cloud up and turn solid, and you will need to bring

them to room temperature before using them. To avoid having to refrigerate, buy oils in small quantities that you can use up in a few weeks.

Onions

Store all dry-skinned onions in a cool, dry place and use before they sprout.

garlic

The most pungent of the onion family. Garlic powder and garlic salt are no substitute for the real thing since they lack the true flavor of garlic.

leeks

Subtle onion flavor, used for soups and in sautés. Leeks keep best in the refrigerator.

red onions

Their sweet flavor makes them ideal for salads. For cooking, they are very mild.

scallions

Also called green onions. Mild flavor. Use the white bulbs as well as the fresh green tops. Wrap in plastic and store in the refrigerator, or chop coarsely, wrap in plastic, and freeze.

shallots

A sweet and delicate cross between onions and garlic. Use chopped for best flavor. Buy the largest you can find because those are easier to peel and chop.

yellow onions

The all-purpose cooking onion; strong flavor—good for flavoring stock.

Rice

long-grain white rice

Lighter and fluffier than short grain when cooked.

wild rice

Technically not a rice, but the seed of a wild grass; nutty in flavor, slightly firm to the bite when properly cooked. Available in most supermarkets and specialty shops, very expensive. But half a pound serves four.

Soy sauce

Buy the Japanese brands, which are very flavorful and less salty than Chinese and American soy sauces.

Sugar

confectioners' sugar
dark brown sugar
granulated sugar
light brown sugar

Tomato products

Italian plum tomatoes

For tomato sauces, canned plum tomatoes are an acceptable substitute for ripe tomatoes and are among the few canned vegetables good cooks will use.

catsup

Useful in small quantities for roasting and barbecuing. (See Judith Olney's oven-barbecued chicken quarters, pages 68–69.)

tomato paste

Also for sauces. With canned paste, spoon out unused portions in one tablespoon amounts onto waxed paper and freeze, then lift the frozen paste off and store in a plastic container. Sometimes available in tubes, which can be refrigerated and kept after a small amount is used.

Vinegars

cider vinegar

Made from apple juice; mild in flavor.

red and white wine vinegars

Made from wines; used in cooking and salad dressings.

sherry wine vinegar

Nutty, and somewhat stronger flavored than most wine vinegars. Buy in specialty stores.

IN THE REFRIGERATOR:

Bread crumbs

You need never buy these. Save stale bread (particularly French loaves), toast it, and make your own bread crumbs in a food processor or blender. Store in a tightly covered jar in the refrigerator, or freeze.

Butter

Unsalted is best for cooking because it does not burn as quickly as salted, and it has a sweeter flavor. Keep frozen until needed.

Cheese, Parmesan

Avoid the preground variety, whether boxed or bottled: it is very expensive and almost flavorless. Buy Parmesan by the half- or quarter-pound wedge and grate as needed: a quarter pound produces one cup of cheese. American Parmesans are acceptable and less costly than imported. Romano is another substitute—or try mixing the two. If you have a specialty cheese shop nearby, ask for Asiago or Kasseri cheeses: less expensive than Parmesan but comparable in flavor and texture.

Coriander

Fresh coriander, usually sold alongside parsley, has similar uses and a hint of orange in its taste. It is commonly called *cilantro* or Chinese parsley. Handle it as you would parsley.

Eggs

Will keep up to six weeks. Before beating eggs, bring them to room temperature for fluffiest results.

Ginger root

Buy fresh in the produce section. Slice only what you need. The rest will stay fresh in the refrigerator for 6 weeks wrapped in plastic. Or place the whole ginger root in a small jar and cover it with dry sherry to preserve it. It will keep indefinitely. You need not peel ginger root.

Lemons

In addition to its many uses in cooking, fresh lemon juice, added to cut fruits and vegetables, keeps them from turning brown. Added to very hot water, lemon juice keeps rice from turning yellow as it cooks. Do not substitute bottled juice or lemon extract. The flavor is quite different and will mar an otherwise perfect dish.

Mustards

Select the pungent Dijon variety for cooking. The flavor survives heating. Dry mustard and regular hot dog mustard have their uses and their devotees, but the recipes in this book call for Dijon. One recipe (page 88) requires coarse mustard, a condiment containing whole mustard seeds. Imported from France and England, coarse mustard, which comes in a small crock and is sold in specialty shops, is good for sandwiches and cold meats.

Parsley

Put in a glass of water and cover loosely with a plastic bag. It will keep for a week in the refrigerator. Or you can wash it, dry it, and refrigerate it in a small plastic bag with a dry paper towel inside to absorb any moisture.

Equipment

Proper cooking equipment makes the work light and is a good cook's most prized possession. You can cook expertly without a store-bought steamer or even a food processor; but basic pans, knives, and a few other items are indispensable. Below are the things you need—and some attractive options—for preparing the menus in this volume.

Pots and pans

2 large skillets, 10-12 inches in diameter, with covers

8-inch skillet with cover

Sauté pan, 10–12 inches in diameter, with cover and oven-proof handle

3 saucepans with covers (1-, 2-, and 4-quart capacities)
> Choose enamel cast iron, plain cast iron, aluminum-clad stainless steel, heavy aluminum, (but you need at least one skillet that is not aluminum). Best—but very expensive— is tin-lined copper.

Double boiler with cover

Two 18-inch shallow baking pans (called jelly-roll pans)

14-inch shallow roasting pan
> Choose aluminum, stainless steel, enamel, or oven-proof glass.

14-inch cookie sheet

3-quart heavy casserole with cover

Knives

> A carbon-steel knife takes a sharp edge but tends to rust. You must wash and dry it after each use; otherwise it can blacken food and counter tops. Good quality stainless-steel knives, frequently honed, are less trouble than carbon steel and will serve just as well in the home kitchen. (Since carbon steel takes an edge more quickly, professional chefs will probably continue to use it.) Never put a fine knife in the dishwasher. Rinse it, dry it, and put it away—but not loose in a drawer. Knives will stay sharp and last long if they have their own storage rack.

Small paring knife (sharp-pointed end)

10- to 12-inch chef's knife

Long bread knife (serrated edge)

Sharpening steel

Knife rack (wall-mounted magnetic kind, or wooden for the counter top)

Other cooking tools

Long-handled cooking spoon

Long-handled slotted spoon

Long-handled wooden spoon

Long-handled, 2-pronged fork

Pair of metal tongs

Wooden spatula (for stirring hot ingredients)

Metal turner (for lifting hot foods from pans)

Rubber or vinyl spatula (for folding hot or cold ingredients, off the heat)

3 mixing bowls in graduated sizes

2 sets of measuring cups and spoons in graduated sizes (one for dry ingredients, another for shortening and liquids)

Strainers (preferably 2, in fine and coarse mesh)

Colander (stainless steel, aluminum, or enamel)

Grater (metal, with several sizes of holes; a rotary grater is handy for hard cheese)

Nutmeg grater

Wooden chopping board

Vegetable peeler

2 wire whisks, 1 large and 1 medium size

Pastry brush for basting (a small, new paintbrush that is not nylon serves well)

Citrus juicer (the inexpensive glass kind from the dime store will do, along with a strainer)

Aluminum foil

Paper towels

Plastic wrap

Waxed paper

Kitchen timer

Roll of masking tape or white paper tape for labeling and dating

Ball of cotton string for trussing

Electric appliances

Blender or food processor
> A blender will do most of the work required in this volume, but a food processor will do it more quickly and in larger volume. Food processors now come in a wide price range and should be considered a necessity, not a luxury, for anyone who enjoys cooking.

Optional

Boning knife

Bulb baster, plastic or metal

Instant-reading meat thermometer

Food mill

Heavy cleaver or meat pounder (for pounding meats)

Metal skewers

Poultry shears

Salad spinner

Vegetable steamer

Zester

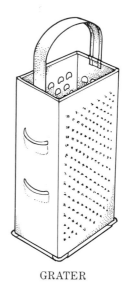

GRATER

VEGETABLE PEELER

IMPROVISED
STEAMER
(Colander in Stockpot)

METAL TURNERS

BULB
BASTER

SAUTE PAN

NUTMEG
GRATER

CITRUS JUICER

PARING KNIFE

BREAD KNIFE

CHEF'S KNIFE

INSTANT-
READING
MEAT
THERMOMETER

DOUBLE BOILER

SHARPENING STEEL

SAUCEPANS

CASSEROLE

SKILLET

BAKING PAN

17

Anne Byrd

One of the richest traditions in American cooking flourishes below the Mason-Dixon line, where for generations good cooks have developed their special ways with chicken, pork, corn, game, and such hot-weather vegetables as okra. A native Southerner and owner of a cooking school in Greensboro, North Carolina, Anne Byrd grew up relishing and mastering the great meals of her region. At the same time, she added her own touches to the best of the down-home recipes, picking up ideas for side dishes, spices, and sauces from other regions of the United States as well as from other nations.

The three menus here reflect this new eclectic kind of cooking. Anne Byrd's fried chicken in the meal at left (see pages 20–21 for recipes) cooks more quickly than older versions. The corn pudding gets a simple but sophisticated dusting of dill or chervil. In Menu 2, where the main dish is flamed chicken, the side dish is bulgur, a vitamin-rich cracked wheat that came to America from the cuisine of the Middle East. Menu 3 centers on a Southern classic—quail. These quail, however, come from the supermarket rather than the woods. Anne Byrd serves them with buttered asparagus and wild rice, which is a native American delicacy from the lake country of Minnesota.

This menu of Southern fried chicken, corn pudding, and sautéed okra is as traditional as a barn raising, but Anne Byrd's approach to old-time Southern cooking produces lighter results that suit modern appetites. The meal looks as good as it tastes, either outdoors on a picnic table, as at left, or in the dining room with bright cotton mats and assorted informal serving pieces to pass around the table.

Southern Fried Chicken
Herbed Corn Pudding
Sautéed Okra with Tomatoes and Herbs

The fried chicken recipe for this menu calls for less fat than the old-fashioned deep fry, and instead of taking an hour or more, the chicken cooks at high temperature in 30 minutes. Buttermilk moistens and flavors the raw chicken before it is dusted with flour.

For authentic deep-South taste, be sure to use lard for the frying, rather than some other oil or fat. The chicken will fry as nicely in vegetable shortening but will not taste the same. You can buy lard, which is rendered pork fat, in pound packages at a butcher shop or the supermarket meat counter. Combining butter with the lard adds flavor too, and the butter will not scorch in this mixture, even at high frying temperatures.

Two timesaving tips: remember to bring the disjointed chicken to room temperature before you cook. It fries faster. Second, create leftovers on purpose: buy two small chickens and fry them in separate skillets. You can handle two chickens almost as easily as one, and the next day you will have a delicious cold lunch.

Because dark meat takes longer to cook, put the legs and thighs in the pan first, then add the breasts, and finally the wings. Remember, too, to use tongs to turn the pieces—a fork pierces the skin and lets the juices run out, leaving the chicken tough and dry.

Freshly picked corn produces the best corn pudding. Buy small to medium-size ears and, after shucking and desilking them, stand each ear on end and cut off the kernels (about three rows at a time) with a sharp knife. Do not slice too deep—the outer half of the kernel is the tastiest. If you cannot find good corn, frozen white "baby" corn is a good alternative. The pudding dish should bake in a pan of boiling water, as the recipe directs. The water keeps the temperature constant so that the texture of the pudding will be smooth.

Okra, a traditional side dish in the summertime, grows only in the South and has to be shipped north. Buy tender pods no more than four inches long. (The larger pods may be slightly wooden in texture.) Okra contains a thick liquid characteristically used to thicken Creole gumbos and stews. To keep it in the pod, where it belongs, avoid cutting off its top (the top is the end that is not pointed). If okra is not in season, buy fresh green beans and stir fry them in the same way.

To peel and seed the tomatoes for the okra recipe, drop them in boiling water for 15 seconds and then drain. Starting at the stem, peel with a paring knife. (The skin will practically slip off without a knife.) Cut the tomato in half and squeeze out the seeds and most of the juice. You will have to use your fingers to remove the remaining seeds. The seeded, dejuiced tomato will provide the right texture and taste for the stir fry but will not liquefy it.

WHAT TO DRINK

Iced tea is an excellent companion for fried chicken. For best results, use tea leaves rather than tea bags. Since you want a strong mixture of tea, allow a heaping tablespoon per glass and use freshly boiled water—about a cup per glass. Steep for five minutes in a teapot and add fresh mint leaves to the brew if you have them. Strain the tea, cool it, and add it to an ice-filled pitcher. Dilute if necessary, add sugar to taste, and serve with lemon slices or wedges. A few mint leaves will look summery in each glass.

If you prefer wine, a good complement to the gentle spicing of this menu would be a dry California Riesling, a white wine with a hint of subdued spice. Serve very cold.

SHOPPING LIST AND STAPLES

2- to 2½-pound chicken, cut into serving pieces
4 ears fresh corn, or 2 cups frozen white corn
¾ pound small pods fresh okra
1 small tomato
1 bunch watercress (optional)
1 bunch fresh parsley
2 teaspoons chopped fresh dill or chervil, or 1 teaspoon dried chervil
1 tablespoon chopped fresh basil, or 1 teaspoon dried
1 small lemon (optional)
⅓ cup buttermilk
1 cup heavy cream
7 tablespoons butter
3 large eggs
⅓ cup lard
½ cup flour
Salt and pepper

UTENSILS

Large deep frying pan
Medium-size skillet
Medium-size saucepan

1½-quart shallow baking dish and larger dish to hold it
Medium-size bowl
Small bowl
Measuring cups and spoons
Chef's knife
All-purpose knife
Whisk
Tongs

START-TO-FINISH STEPS

1. Cut chicken into serving pieces. Cut kernels from corn ears for corn pudding. Trim okra and chop tomato for okra recipe. Chop herbs for okra and corn pudding.
2. Follow corn pudding recipe steps 1 through 7. While pudding bakes, follow chicken recipe steps 1 through 8.
3. Follow okra recipe steps 1 through 3.
4. Follow corn pudding recipe step 8.
5. Wedge lemon and follow chicken recipe step 9.
6. Serve okra and corn pudding with chicken.

RECIPES

Southern Fried Chicken

2- to 2½-pound chicken, cut into serving pieces
½ cup flour
⅓ cup buttermilk
⅓ cup lard
5 tablespoons butter
1½ teaspoons salt
½ teaspoon freshly ground black pepper
Lemon wedges and watercress for garnish (optional)

1. Rinse chicken pieces and pat dry with paper towels.
2. Put flour in paper bag.
3. Pour buttermilk into medium-size bowl and dip each chicken piece in it to coat. Place 1 or 2 chicken pieces in bag and shake to coat with flour. Place coated pieces of chicken on plate. Repeat until all chicken pieces are floured.
4. Melt lard and butter over high heat in frying pan.
5. Meanwhile, sprinkle chicken with salt and pepper.
6. When fat is hot, add thighs and legs, fleshy side down. Brown about 3 minutes. When golden, turn them with tongs and brown other sides. Add chicken breasts to pan. After about 3 more minutes, turn all chicken pieces. Add wings to pan.
7. Continue cooking and turning chicken pieces so that they brown evenly. Cook chicken on as high a temperature as possible. Reduce temperature to medium-high only if chicken is browning too fast. It should be done in 20 to 30 minutes from time thighs and legs were placed in pan. Chicken should be medium brown and the crust very crisp.
8. Spread doubled paper towels on warm serving platter and place chicken on top; then cover chicken with doubled paper towels. Allow chicken to drain 3 to 5 minutes in a warm spot. Remove towels.
9. Garnish chicken platter with lemon wedges and watercress, if desired.

Herbed Corn Pudding

2 cups kernels cut from 4 ears fresh corn, or frozen white corn, defrosted
2 teaspoons chopped fresh dill or chervil, or 1 teaspoon dried chervil
3 large eggs
1 teaspoon salt
1 cup heavy cream
Additional chopped fresh dill for garnish (optional)

1. Preheat oven to 350 degrees.
2. Bring water to a boil to pour around baking dish.
3. Place corn kernels in lightly greased shallow baking dish and sprinkle dill on top.
4. Using whisk, beat eggs about 10 strokes in small bowl. Add salt and cream and beat to incorporate.
5. Pour custard over corn and dill and stir briefly.
6. Place baking dish with corn pudding in larger dish. Pour enough boiling water into larger dish so that water comes about halfway up side of pudding dish.
7. Place dishes on middle rack of oven. Bake 35 to 40 minutes, or until knife inserted 1½ inches in from edge of baking dish comes out clean. The center will set after pudding is removed from oven.
8. Garnish with additional chopped fresh dill, if desired.

Sautéed Okra with Tomatoes and Herbs

2 tablespoons butter
¾ pound small pods fresh okra, rinsed and dried, with stems, but not end of pod, cut off
¼ teaspoon salt
1 small tomato, peeled, seeded, and chopped
1 tablespoon chopped fresh basil, or 1 teaspoon dried
1 tablespoon chopped fresh parsley

1. Melt butter in skillet over high heat.
2. Sauté okra 3 to 5 minutes, depending on size of pods. Stir okra frequently so that pods do not brown. They should be just tender and bright green.
3. Remove okra to warm serving platter and sprinkle with salt. Top with chopped tomato and herbs.

ADDED TOUCH

If you serve the meal in the backyard or on the patio, watermelon slices or assorted flavors of ice cream make the easiest and most appropriate desserts. The blueberry cobbler on page 27 is another possibility. Serve it warm and top each portion off with vanilla ice cream.

LEFTOVER SUGGESTIONS

Fried chicken is especially good the second day, when allowed to warm to room temperature. If any okra and tomato sauté is left over, it will make a nice addition in tomorrow morning's omelet.

Flamed Chicken with Mushrooms
Bulgur with Aromatic Vegetables
Tomatoes with Chopped Herbs

Mushrooms, chicken breasts, and bulgur make a rich, dark dish that looks even better if enhanced with a bright salad. In summer use fresh tomatoes and in winter an assortment of watercress and two or three other, paler greens.

The bulgur that goes with the brandy-flamed chicken breasts in this menu is simply unbleached cracked wheat with all the good flavor of whole-grain bread. Look for it in the supermarket next to the rice, dried beans, or breakfast cereals. Health food stores and specialty shops often sell it loose, by the pound. Buy an unrefined brand, since the nutrients are mostly in the dark husk.

During cooking, the wine and brandy in the sauce lose their alcoholic content but not their flavor. When you cook with wine or spirits, therefore, always use something that you consider genuinely fit to drink. Your guests and family will enjoy watching you flame the chicken, so invite them into the kitchen or finish the dish at the table if you are serving in the dining room. Unless the brandy is warm, it will not catch fire. Warm it on the stove for a moment before you bring it in, then ignite it with a match. Or warm it over a small open-flame burner at the table. Remember that the brandy may accidentally flame up without your putting a match to it. If so, you should cover the pan with a lid, taking care to stand at arm's length.

WHAT TO DRINK

A bright, slightly acidic white wine will make a nice counterpoint to the rich flavors of this menu. Try an Italian Pinot Grigio or Pinot Bianco from either Friuli or Trentino-Alto Adige. Whichever you select, buy enough to use in the sauce as well as at dinner.

If you prefer a Mideastern touch, in keeping with the bulgur, brew hot tea with mint leaves and sugar.

SHOPPING LIST AND STAPLES

8 skinless, boneless chicken breast halves
4 large shallots
½ pound fresh mushrooms
1 carrot
1 stalk celery
1 small onion
4 tomatoes
1 bunch fresh parsley
1 tablespoon chopped fresh marjoram, or 1 teaspoon dried
2 tablespoons chopped fresh basil, or 2 teaspoons dried
2 tablespoons chopped fresh chives, or 2 teaspoons freeze-dried
8 tablespoons butter (1 stick)
1 cup bulgur

1½ cups chicken broth
Salt and pepper
¼ cup dry white wine
¼ cup brandy

UTENSILS

Large skillet
Medium-size saucepan
Small saucepan
Measuring cups and spoons
Heavy cleaver or meat pounder
Chef's knife
Paring knife
Tongs
Waxed paper

START-TO-FINISH STEPS

1. Chop herbs, mushrooms, and shallots for chicken recipe. Chop vegetables and herbs for bulgur recipe. Chop herbs for tomato recipe.
2. Follow tomato recipe steps 1 through 4.
3. Follow bulgur recipe steps 1 through 4.
4. Follow chicken recipe steps 1 through 7.
5. Follow bulgur recipe step 5.
6. Follow tomato recipe step 5.
7. Serve chicken and bulgur with tomatoes.

RECIPES

Flamed Chicken with Mushrooms

5 tablespoons butter
¼ cup minced shallots
½ pound fresh mushrooms, sliced
1 tablespoon chopped fresh marjoram, or 1 teaspoon dried
2 tablespoons chopped fresh chives, or 2 teaspoons freeze-dried
Salt and freshly ground black pepper
¼ cup dry white wine
8 skinless, boneless chicken breast halves
¼ cup brandy
2 tablespoons chopped fresh parsley for garnish (optional)

1. Melt 3 tablespoons of the butter in skillet large enough to hold chicken in one layer. (It may be necessary to use two skillets to cook chicken.) Stir in shallots and cook over low heat for about a minute.
2. Add mushrooms and continue cooking for another minute. Stir in herbs, seasonings, and wine. Cook over moderately high heat about 3 minutes, or until wine has reduced to an essence.
3. Remove mushroom mixture and set aside on warm plate. Cover and keep warm.
4. Put chicken between sheets of waxed paper and pound until breasts are about ½ inch thick. Season with salt and pepper.

5. Add the remaining 2 tablespoons butter to skillet over medium-high heat. When butter is hot, sauté chicken breasts, without crowding pan, 3 to 4 minutes on 1 side until lightly browned. Reduce heat slightly, turn each breast with tongs, and brown other side—adding more butter if necessary. Place some mushroom mixture on top of each breast and turn off heat.
6. Slightly warm brandy in small saucepan. Standing back, hold a match just above brandy and set it aflame.
7. Pour flaming brandy over chicken. Shake pan gently until flames have subsided. Remove to platter and garnish with parsley, if desired.

Bulgur with Aromatic Vegetables

3 tablespoons butter
¼ cup chopped carrots
¼ cup chopped celery
¼ cup chopped onion
1 cup bulgur
1½ cups chicken broth
¼ teaspoon salt
2 tablespoons chopped fresh parsley

1. Melt butter over medium heat and add chopped vegetables. Cook, stirring, for 1 minute.
2. Add bulgur and toss for 3 to 5 minutes until vegetables have softened and bulgur is golden brown.
3. Add chicken broth and salt and bring to a boil.
4. Reduce heat to medium low. Simmer, uncovered, about 15 minutes, or until all liquid has been absorbed.
5. Stir in chopped parsley.

Tomatoes with Chopped Herbs

4 tomatoes
2 tablespoons chopped fresh parsley
2 tablespoons chopped fresh basil, or 2 teaspoons dried
Salt and freshly ground black pepper

1. Bring enough water to a boil to cover tomatoes.
2. Drop tomatoes into boiling water for about 15 seconds.
3. Drain tomatoes. With paring knife, slip off their skins.
4. Slice tomatoes and arrange on platter. Refrigerate.
5. Before serving, top tomatoes with chopped herbs and season with salt and pepper.

ADDED TOUCH

For a quick dessert, chill a honeydew melon and, just before serving, cut into slices. Then run a sharp knife between the melon and the rind and cut the melon into bite-size pieces. Garnish with fresh sprigs of mint.

LEFTOVER SUGGESTION

The bulgur-and-vegetable mixture makes a good cold dish, and you will find it worthwhile to double the recipe and have leftovers. Toss it lightly with a vinaigrette dressing and garnish it with tomato wedges.

Sautéed Quail
Steamed Asparagus with Chervil Butter
Herbed Wild Rice

Silver serving pieces, if you have them, or your other best dishes and tablecloth, will underline the elegance of sautéed *quail, wild rice, and fresh asparagus. Garnish the main dish with sprigs of parsley or with thin-sliced lemon, or both.*

In the South, where quail was once a favorite dish at fancy lunches, the preferred breed was the bobwhite, one of three recognized varieties. Bobwhite are now a protected game bird, to be hunted only for a few weeks in the fall. Almost identical in every respect, however, are commercially grown quail now available in most fine meat stores. They grow to full size (five or six ounces each) and are ready for market six to eight weeks after hatching. If you cannot find quail at your local market, ask the butcher to stock them or write Manchester Farms (one of the largest breeders) at Box 97, Dalzell, South Carolina 29040, for the nearest distributor in your area.

Quail, which are all white meat and virtually fat free, are so small that you must allow two per serving. Generally more flavorful than chicken, they cook very fast. Over cooking will spoil their flavor and even their looks, for if they are baked or roasted too long, they fall apart. This recipe calls for sautéing the birds about 20 minutes, an ideal technique, and then coating them with a bourbon-accented cream sauce. Because they are so small, they are hard to eat without using your fingers, particularly for the leg and thigh meat.

Wild rice, like quail, is a special occasion dish—and the two blend deliciously. Technically not a true rice, this nutty-flavored grain is a wild grass seed and is one of many American contributions to world cuisine. Originally harvested wild by Indians, it grows only in Wisconsin, Minnesota, a few other northern states, and Canada. Commercial growers now successfully cultivate it, but the crop is always small, and wild rice sells for about 10 dollars a pound. Fortunately, one cup of raw rice (equal to one half pound) yields enough for four. You can find wild rice in most supermarkets and specialty shops. Be sure the package you choose is not a combination of wild rice and regular white rice.

A sauce of butter and chervil complements the fresh asparagus in this menu. Chervil is a delicate herb that combines the flavors of parsley, dill, and a hint of anise. Dried chervil, sold in many supermarkets, is not as good as fresh, but it will do. And, if you enjoy gardening, remember that chervil is one of the easiest herbs to grow. Plant it either in full sun indoors or partial sunlight outdoors. Dried and put into jars, chervil keeps well over the winter, and you can also freeze it in small packets—really a better method of preserving chervil than drying it. The plant is a perennial. Whether you grow it or buy it, be sure to add chervil at the last moment before finishing and serving the dish. Heat destroys it.

If fresh asparagus is not in season, substitute fresh green beans or broccoli, either of which will combine deliciously with the chervil butter sauce.

WHAT TO DRINK

The special flavor of asparagus unfortunately acts to distort the flavor of many wines, but in this case the quail and the wild rice win out. For a meal that is this festive, the best choice would almost certainly be a French Champagne: a nonvintage brut, served very cold and kept on ice during the dinner.

SHOPPING LIST AND STAPLES

8 fresh or frozen quail
1 large onion
1 pound fresh asparagus
1 bunch fresh parsley
1 tablespoon chopped fresh chervil, or 1 teaspoon dried
1 tablespoon chopped fresh chives, or 1 teaspoon
   freeze-dried
1 tablespoon chopped fresh thyme, or 1 teaspoon dried
10 tablespoons butter (1¼ sticks)
1½ cups chicken broth
1 cup wild rice
2 tablespoons flour
Salt and pepper
1 cup bourbon

UTENSILS

Large skillet
Large sauté pan
Vegetable steamer
Medium-size saucepan with cover
Small saucepan
Measuring cups and spoons
All-purpose knife
Poultry shears
Whisk
Tongs

START-TO-FINISH STEPS

1. Chop onion for quail recipe. Chop herbs for asparagus

and rice recipes.

2. Follow rice recipe steps 1 through 3.

3. Follow asparagus recipe steps 1 through 3. As asparagus steams, follow quail recipe steps 1 through 3.

4. Follow asparagus recipe step 4.

5. Follow quail recipe steps 4 through 7.

6. Follow asparagus recipe step 5.

7. Follow quail recipe step 8 and serve with rice and asparagus.

RECIPES

Sautéed Quail

8 fresh quail, or 8 frozen quail, thoroughly defrosted
Salt and freshly ground black pepper
4 tablespoons butter
½ cup plus ⅓ cup bourbon
½ cup finely chopped onions
2 tablespoons flour
1½ cups chicken broth
Sprigs of parsley (optional)

1. Split quail with poultry shears down their backs, and spread open. Sprinkle lightly with salt and pepper.

2. Taking care not to let it burn, melt butter over high heat in sauté pan. Place quail, flesh side down, in hot butter and sauté 3 minutes. Turn and sauté on other side 3 minutes more, or until both sides are golden.

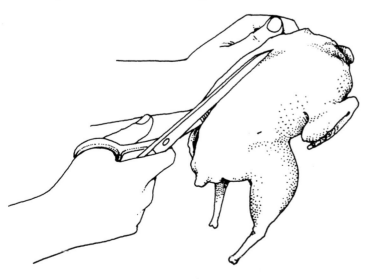

Using poultry shears, cut quail down the backbone.

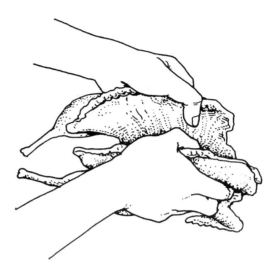

Spread each bird flat, with backbones outward.

3. Slightly warm ½ cup of the bourbon in small saucepan. Standing back, hold a match just above bourbon and set it aflame. With quail off heat, carefully pour flaming bourbon over quail.

4. Reduce heat to medium. Turn birds again, flesh side down, and cook 7 minutes. Turn flesh side up and cook 7 more minutes.

5. Remove quail to warm serving platter and place in 200-degree oven to keep warm.

6. Set heat under sauté pan to medium high. With whisk, stir chopped onions into juices in pan and cook 2 to 3 minutes. Whisk flour into mixture. Whisk the remaining ⅓ cup bourbon and chicken broth into flour mixture. Bring to a boil, stirring frequently.

7. When sauce has thickened, remove from heat. Taste and season with salt and pepper.

8. Lightly coat quail with sauce and serve the remaining sauce separately; garnish with parsley, if desired.

Steamed Asparagus with Chervil Butter

1 pound fresh asparagus
4 tablespoons butter
1 tablespoon chopped fresh chervil, or 1 teaspoon dried
½ teaspoon salt

1. Wash asparagus and trim stalks.

2. Fill vegetable steamer with water to just below steamer rack. Place asparagus in steamer and steam, covered, 8 to 15 minutes, depending on size of stalks.

3. Test asparagus stalks with tines of fork. When they are tender, but still resist with slight crunch, remove asparagus from heat.

4. Plunge asparagus into cold water to stop cooking and to set color. Drain and set aside until 5 minutes before serving.
5. Melt butter in skillet. Add asparagus and toss in hot butter. Add chervil and salt. Serve immediately.

Herbed Wild Rice

2 tablespoons butter
¼ cup chopped onion
1 cup wild rice
1 tablespoon chopped fresh parsley
1 tablespoon chopped fresh chives, or 1 teaspoon
  freeze-dried
1 tablespoon chopped fresh thyme, or 1 teaspoon dried
½ teaspoon salt
Freshly ground black pepper
2½ cups water

1. In medium-size saucepan, melt butter over medium-high heat. Add onion and cook about 2 minutes until soft.
2. Stir in wild rice and mix until coated with butter. Add parsley, herbs, salt, pepper, and water.
3. Bring mixture to a boil. Reduce heat to medium-low and cook, covered, 30 to 35 minutes, or until all liquid has been absorbed, and kernels are tender but still have some crunch. Keep warm until serving time.

ADDED TOUCHES

For a celebratory dinner you may want to take a few extra minutes to make a special dessert. To accompany quail, Anne Byrd serves either iced lemon cream or blueberry cobbler. An advantage of the iced lemon cream is that you can make it any time. It keeps a month in the freezer. Make the blueberry cobbler ahead on the same day and warm it before serving.

Iced Lemon Cream

4 egg yolks
½ cup sugar
Zest of 1 lemon, chopped or cut into julienne strips
Juice of 1 large lemon
1 cup heavy cream
Lemon twists for garnish (optional)

1. Beat yolks and sugar with electric mixer about 2 minutes.
2. Add lemon zest (outer rind) and juice, and beat another minute to incorporate.
3. In another bowl, whip cream. When it reaches same consistency as yolk mixture, pour yolks into cream and beat together about 1 minute. Scrape beaters to remove any lemon zest and stir back into cream.
4. Pour ¾ to 1 cup of the mixture into individual serving bowls and place in freezer for at least 1 hour. If you freeze the cream for more than a few hours, cover bowls with foil. Before serving, allow it to soften slightly in refrigerator.
5. At serving time, garnish with lemon twists, if desired.

Blueberry Cobbler

If using fresh blueberries for the cobbler, treat them gently, washing them in running water in a colander and then picking over them carefully to remove the stems. You should make the cobbler as near meal time as possible, because it is best served warm. Whip a pint of cream to top it off, or serve it with vanilla ice cream.

1 pint fresh blueberries (about 2 cups), or frozen unsweetened blueberries, well drained
⅔ cup sugar
1 lemon
1 cup flour, plus ¼ cup if using frozen blueberries
1 teaspoon baking powder
¼ teaspoon baking soda
¼ teaspoon salt
6 tablespoons butter
½ cup buttermilk

1. Preheat oven to 400 degrees.
2. Rinse and pick over blueberries. Thoroughly drain. Place them in greased 1½-quart baking dish and sprinkle ⅓ cup of the sugar on top, plus ¼ cup of the flour if using frozen blueberries.
3. Cut off zest of lemon, not bitter white part. Cut zest into very thin strips and sprinkle on top of blueberries.
4. Cut lemon in half and squeeze juice (about three tablespoons) through sieve over berries. Stir gently to combine berries with sugar and lemon mixture.
5. Sift the remaining 1 cup flour, the remaining ⅓ cup sugar, baking powder, baking soda, and salt into bowl.
6. Cut butter into flour mixture until coarse and crumbly.
7. Add buttermilk and stir until blended. Beat with spoon about 30 seconds, or until dough sticks together.
8. Spread dough on top of blueberries. Do not worry if there are holes; they will fill in as cobbler bakes.
9. Bake 1 hour, or until golden brown.

Perla Meyers

P erla Meyers grew up in Catalonia, the north-eastern region of Spain, which used to be an independent kingdom and still has its traditional cuisine. She learned to cook from the family cook, who was Spanish, as well as from her Alsatian-born father and her Viennese mother. From them she acquired the habit of cooking by the season, choosing a main course, vegetables, and salads only after a trip to the market to see what is freshest and best.

She likes to begin a meal with a vegetable appetizer, such as the cauliflower vinaigrette at right—a custom in Catalonia as well as in other Mediterranean regions. A vegetable first course not only satisfies the appetite but also makes sense for the busy cook, since not all the dishes need to be ready at the same time. The cook and the guests can enjoy the first course while the main dish finishes or stays warm for a few minutes.

Today Perla Meyers continues to borrow techniques and ideas from abroad. The chicken breasts sautéed with sausage and zucchini in Menu 1 is a Basque dish—from northwestern Spain. In Menu 2, which offers a sauté of chicken and mushrooms as the main course, the salad is an Italian mix of zucchini, tuna, and tomato. And the green peppercorn sauce in Menu 3 is originally French.

This family meal will turn out best when cauliflower and zucchini are at their peak, in late summer and early fall. You can serve the cauliflower appetizer as a first course, garnished with cherry tomatoes, salami, and black olives. Then bring on the sliced chicken breasts cooked with sweet Italian sausages, red pepper, and sliced zucchini, and—to fill out the meal—a lemony rice pilaf and perhaps French bread.

Cauliflower with Roquefort Vinaigrette
Basque Sauté of Chicken Breasts
Creamy Lemon Pilaf

For the hors d'oeuvre, choose the whitest cauliflower you can find, avoiding any spotted or yellowish heads or any with open flower clusters. The recipe calls for a cup of milk to be added to the cooking water with the cauliflower. This keeps the cauliflower white without changing the taste. The oil-cured black olives, which are imported, are not as salty as those packed in salt and brine.

Crème fraîche, an increasingly popular ingredient in American kitchens, is very different from plain sweet cream or commercial sour cream. A staple of French cooking, it is a raw cream that has matured naturally and is slightly sour tasting. Look for *crème fraîche* in the dairy department. It will cost more than sour cream, which you may also opt for in the cauliflower recipe, but is worth trying. Leftover *crème fraîche* has many uses—as a topping for fresh fruit, cakes, or baked potatoes.

For the Basque sauté of chicken, you may want to roast your own red peppers rather than buying them in a jar. If so, select one large, unblemished pepper. To skin it, set it on a low flame on range top (or under the broiler of an electric oven if you do not have a gas stove), and allow the skin to blacken in the heat. Remove the blackened skin, core the pepper, and chop it.

WHAT TO DRINK

The strong flavors of this menu call for a wine with enough body to support them. Choose a not-too-expensive, white Graves, a California Sauvignon Blanc (sometimes labeled Fumé Blanc), or a white Spanish wine from the Rioja region.

SHOPPING LIST AND STAPLES

4 skinless, boneless chicken breast halves
¾ pound sweet Italian sausages
¼ pound Genoa salami, thinly sliced (optional)
1 large head cauliflower
1 pint cherry tomatoes (optional)
2 medium-size zucchini
1 hot dried chili pepper or crushed red pepper (optional)
3 large cloves garlic
3 tablespoons minced fresh chives, or 1 tablespoon
　　freeze-dried
1 bunch fresh parsley
1 lemon
2 ounces Roquefort cheese

¼ pound Parmesan cheese
2 tablespoons *crème fraîche* or sour cream
¼ cup heavy cream
1 cup milk
3 tablespoons butter
2 extra-large eggs
3⅓ cups chicken broth
2 or 3 anchovy fillets (optional)
7-ounce jar roasted peppers
½ pound oil-cured black olives (optional)
¾ cup olive oil
3 tablespoons sherry wine vinegar or red wine vinegar
1½ cups long-grain white rice
½ cup flour
Salt and pepper
¼ cup dry white wine

UTENSILS

Blender or food processor
Large skillet with cover
Heavy saucepan
Large saucepan with cover
Small bowl
Measuring cups and spoons
Chef's knife
All-purpose knife
Rubber spatula
Slotted spoon
Grater
Tongs
Whisk
Waxed paper
Juicer

START-TO-FINISH STEPS

1. Mince chives for Roquefort vinaigrette. Slice zucchini and garlic for chicken recipe. Grate Parmesan cheese for pilaf recipe.
2. Follow vinaigrette recipe steps 1 and 2.
3. Juice lemon and follow lemon-cream sauce recipe.
4. Follow chicken recipe step 1.
5. Follow pilaf recipe steps 1 and 2.
6. Follow cauliflower recipe steps 1 and 2.
7. Follow chicken recipe steps 2 through 6.
8. Follow cauliflower recipe step 3 and serve cauliflower

with Roquefort vinaigrette as the first course.

9. Follow pilaf recipe step 3 and serve with chicken.

RECIPES

Cauliflower

2½ quarts salted water
1 large head cauliflower
1 cup milk
Roquefort vinaigrette (see following recipe)
¼ pound Genoa salami, thinly sliced for garnish (optional)
½ pound oil-cured black olives for garnish (optional)
1 pint cherry tomatoes for garnish (optional)
Parsley sprigs for garnish (optional)

1. In large covered saucepan, bring 2½ quarts salted water to a boil.
2. Trim cauliflower. Add cauliflower and milk to boiling water. Cook over medium heat 8 minutes, or until cauliflower is crisp but tender. Test by inserting blade of knife near core end—it should come out easily.
3. Remove and drain cauliflower. Place on round serving platter. Serve with Roquefort vinaigrette and surround with salami, black olives, cherry tomatoes, and parsley as desired.

Roquefort Vinaigrette

1 large clove garlic, mashed
½ cup olive oil
2 ounces Roquefort cheese
3 tablespoons sherry wine vinegar or red wine vinegar
2 tablespoons *crème fraîche* or sour cream
2 or 3 rinsed anchovy fillets (optional)
Freshly ground black pepper
3 tablespoons minced fresh chives, or 1 tablespoon
  freeze-dried

1. Combine all ingredients except pepper and chives, including anchovy fillets if desired, in container of blender or food processor and blend until smooth. Season carefully with pepper. You will probably not need salt since both Roquefort and anchovies are salty.
2. Using rubber spatula, stir minced chives into dressing and set aside until serving time. Stir again just before serving and spoon over cauliflower.

Basque Sauté of Chicken Breasts

4 skinless, boneless chicken breast halves
Salt and freshly ground pepper
½ cup flour
2 to 4 tablespoons olive oil
2 medium-size zucchini, cut into 1½-inch matchsticks
¾ pound sweet Italian sausages
1 tablespoon butter
1 hot dried chili pepper, or ½ teaspoon crushed red
  pepper (optional)
¼ cup dry white wine
2 large cloves garlic, thinly sliced
⅓ cup chicken broth

7-ounce jar roasted peppers, drained and finely sliced
1 tablespoon finely chopped fresh parsley

1. Remove fillets (see page 8, step 7) from chicken breasts and remove and discard all fat and gristle. Cut chicken breasts crosswise into ½-inch slices. Season with salt and pepper and dredge lightly in flour. Set aside.
2. Place skillet over high heat. Add 2 tablespoons olive oil to skillet and, when hot, add zucchini. Sauté zucchini 3 minutes, or until nicely browned. Season with salt and pepper, remove with slotted spoon, and reserve.
3. Add sausages and sauté over medium heat until nicely browned on all sides. Add more oil if needed. When done, remove sausages and set aside. Discard all but 1 tablespoon of the fat from skillet.
4. Add butter and hot chili to skillet. When fat is hot, add chicken slices and sauté them over high heat 2 to 3 minutes, until browned. Add wine to skillet, bring to a boil, stir, and reduce for 2 to 3 minutes.
5. Add garlic and broth and simmer chicken, partly covered, 2 to 3 minutes more.
6. Slice sausages crosswise into ¼-inch slices. Add sausage slices, zucchini, and roasted red peppers to skillet. Toss with chicken and simmer over low heat 2 to 3 minutes. Taste for seasoning and sprinkle with chopped parsley.

Creamy Lemon Pilaf

2 tablespoons butter
1½ cups long-grain white rice
3 cups chicken broth
Salt
Lemon-cream sauce (see following recipe)
3 tablespoons freshly grated Parmesan cheese
3 tablespoons finely chopped parsley
Freshly ground black pepper

1. Heat butter in heavy saucepan.
2. Add rice and cook 1 minute, or until rice turns opaque. Add chicken broth and season with salt. Bring to a boil, reduce heat, and simmer, covered, 20 to 25 minutes.
3. Just before serving, add lemon-cream sauce to rice and fold in gently. Add Parmesan cheese and parsley. Taste, and season with salt and pepper. Serve immediately.

Lemon-Cream Sauce

1 tablespoon lemon juice
1 teaspoon grated lemon peel
2 yolks from extra-large eggs
¼ cup heavy cream

Combine lemon juice, lemon peel, yolks, and cream in small bowl. Whisk until well blended. Reserve for rice.

ADDED TOUCH

For a light, sweet dessert, chill, peel, and thinly slice four oranges. Sprinkle a teaspoon of orange liqueur (Grand Marnier and Triple Sec are both good with oranges) and a teaspoon of confectioners' sugar over each portion.

Zucchini, Tuna, and Tomato Salad
Sauté of Chicken with Mushrooms
Broccoli Puree

The right season for this meal is late summer, when the tomatoes and zucchini in the first-course salad are at their peak. The chicken and mushroom sauté with a cream sauce arrives at table with an appetizing-looking broccoli puree.

Y ou can make the sauté of chicken dark meat with mushrooms in any season, since the mushrooms here are dried. The broccoli, pureed to accompany the chicken, is also available year around. But the first course of this menu, which comes from northern Italy, depends upon the perfection of the zucchini and the tomatoes. Tuna packed in olive oil is another essential.

WHAT TO DRINK

Because of the fine textures of this meal, a light white wine would taste too acidic. Try instead a fuller wine, perhaps a white Burgundy from the Macon region or a moderately priced California Chardonnay—and serve lightly chilled.

SHOPPING LIST AND STAPLES

6 to 8 small chicken legs with thighs
1 bunch broccoli (about 1½ pounds)
3 small zucchini
1 pint cherry tomatoes
1 medium-size red onion
2 small yellow onions
1 green pepper
1 large clove garlic
1 bunch fresh parsley
¾ cup heavy cream
½ to ¾ cup sour cream
8 tablespoons butter (1 stick)
2 eggs (optional)
1½ cups chicken broth
7½-ounce can light tuna in olive oil
2 small dill gherkins
1 ounce Italian dried mushrooms
1 teaspoon vegetable oil
½ cup plus 1 tablespoon olive oil
3 tablespoons sherry wine vinegar or red wine vinegar
4 tablespoons flour
Coarse (kosher) salt
Salt and pepper

UTENSILS

Food processor
Large heavy skillet with cover
Small skillet
Large saucepan

32

Medium-size saucepan
Small saucepan with cover
Salad bowl
Small bowl
Measuring cups and spoons
All-purpose knife
Slotted spoon
Vegetable peeler
Whisk
Tongs

START-TO-FINISH STEPS

In the morning: hard-boil eggs for zucchini recipe, if egg garnish is desired.

1. Follow chicken recipe step 1. While mushrooms simmer, follow zucchini recipe steps 1 through 3.
2. Peel and cut onions for chicken recipe.
3. Follow chicken recipe steps 2 and 3. As chicken sautés, follow broccoli recipe steps 1 through 5.
4. Follow chicken recipe step 4.
5. Serve zucchini salad as the first course, followed by chicken and broccoli.

RECIPES

Zucchini, Tuna, and Tomato Salad

3 small zucchini
7½-ounce can light tuna in olive oil
½ cup thinly sliced red onions
½ green pepper, seeded and thinly sliced
2 small dill gherkins, thinly sliced
1 pint cherry tomatoes
Coarse (kosher) salt and freshly ground black pepper
1 large clove garlic, mashed
3 tablespoons sherry wine vinegar or red wine vinegar
½ cup plus 1 tablespoon olive oil
2 tablespoons finely chopped fresh parsley for garnish
    (optional)
2 sliced hard-boiled eggs for garnish (optional)

1. In medium-size saucepan, bring about 1 cup salted water to a boil. Add zucchini and poach 5 minutes, or until barely tender. Remove, cool under cold water, and slice thinly.
2. In salad bowl, combine zucchini, flaked tuna with its oil, onion, green pepper, and gherkins. Slice cherry tomatoes in half and add to bowl. Season with coarse salt and freshly ground black pepper.
3. Combine mashed garlic, vinegar, and olive oil in small bowl and blend thoroughly. Toss dressing with salad ingredients. Serve at room temperature or slightly chilled. Garnish with chopped parsley and hard-boiled egg slices, if desired.

Sauté of Chicken with Mushrooms

1 ounce Italian dried mushrooms
1½ cups chicken broth

6 to 8 small chicken legs with thighs
Salt and freshly ground black pepper
4 tablespoons butter
1 teaspoon vegetable oil
2 small yellow onions, cut in half crosswise
1 tablespoon flour
¾ cup heavy cream
Finely minced fresh parsley for garnish (optional)

1. Rinse mushrooms quickly under cold running water. Combine in small saucepan with 1 cup of the chicken broth. Bring to a boil. Reduce heat, cover, and simmer 20 minutes. Drain mushrooms, reserving liquid; dice them and set aside.
2. Rinse chicken pieces and dry thoroughly with paper towels. Season with salt and pepper. In large heavy skillet, heat 3 tablespoons of the butter with oil. Sauté chicken on both sides until it is nicely browned. Do not crowd pan.
3. Add onions to skillet and pour in ¼ cup of the remaining chicken broth. Lower heat and simmer, partially covered, 25 to 30 minutes, turning chicken once. Add some of the mushroom liquid if needed. Be sure not to drown chicken, or it will lose its nice color.
4. When chicken is done, use tongs to remove it from skillet and set it aside on platter. Remove onions with slotted spoon and discard.
5. Skim surface of pan juices of any fat. Add mushrooms and the remaining ¼ cup chicken broth to skillet. Cook until sauce is reduced to ½ cup.
6. Make *beurre manié* by combining flour with the remaining 1 tablespoon butter, working it together with your fingers until thoroughly blended.
7. Add cream to reduced sauce. Taste and season carefully with salt and pepper. Whisk in a little *beurre manié* until sauce is just thick enough to heavily coat spoon.
8. Return chicken to skillet and coat with sauce. Reheat, and serve garnished with parsley, if desired.

Broccoli Puree

1 bunch broccoli (about 1½ pounds)
4 tablespoons butter
3 tablespoons flour
½ to ¾ cup sour cream
Salt and freshly ground black pepper

1. Remove all leaves from broccoli stalks. Peel stalks with vegetable peeler or sharp knife and cut broccoli into 1-inch pieces.
2. In large saucepan, bring salted water to a boil. Add broccoli and cook 7 to 8 minutes, until tender.
3. Drain thoroughly and puree in food processor.
4. In small skillet, heat butter. Add flour and cook mixture, whisking constantly, until it turns pale brown. Add brown butter to broccoli puree, together with ½ cup sour cream, and stir to blend. If puree seems too thick, add a little more sour cream. Taste and correct seasoning.
5. Transfer to shallow covered serving dish. Keep warm in 200-degree oven until ready to serve.

Game Hens with Green Peppercorn Sauce
Sweet and Sour Turnips
Green Salad with Lemon Mustard Vinaigrette

Sweet and sour turnips, glazed with pan juices, match the golden tones of roasted game hens, which you untruss and cut in half before saucing and serving. A two-green salad and a bright table setting make the meal even more inviting.

Game hens need herbs, seasonings, and care. Here Perla Meyers combines them with rosemary, thyme, paprika, mustard, and green peppercorns—which are pepper berries picked before they ripen and turn black. Jars of green peppercorns preserved in brine or vinegar are on the shelf in most supermarkets and specialty shops. Always buy the brine-packed kind because vinegar overwhelms the peppery flavor. Be sure to add green peppercorns to the sauce at the last minute.

Take time to truss the game hens before you roast them: see the trussing diagrams on the following page. A trussed hen is easier for the cook to turn. And because the skin stays whole and the legs will cook close to the body, a trussed bird will look better after it has been untrussed and carved.

Small white turnips, far from being bitter, taste like a cross between a tart apple and radish: they hold their own in a full-flavored meal such as this one. They have a firm, clean texture, if not over cooked. Avoid large turnips, which do tend to turn woody and bitter.

Salad tip: most produce markets cut off turnip tops and discard them, but fresh green turnip tops make an interesting addition to any green salad, including the Boston lettuce and spinach salad in the recipe here.

Also known as butterhead, Boston lettuce is pale and leafy and a perfect companion to deep-green spinach. The whole head should be loosely packed when you buy Boston lettuce; also, check the inside leaves to make sure they are light yellow. Look for very green leaves that are not split or damaged. If bagged spinach is the only kind available, buy a bag that springs back to the touch.

Buy the greens the day you serve them and wash them just before assembling the salad. Boston lettuce needs only two or three washings, but you must wash spinach with special care in order to remove all grit. First cut off the stems, then fill a large pan or bowl with water and immerse the greens. Rinse and drain at least three times, and taste a leaf. If necessary, rinse again. Drain the spinach on paper towels and pat it dry. A salad spinner will save trouble and cut preparation time. In any case, be sure to dry the leaves thoroughly, for otherwise the dressing will not cling and the salad will taste watery.

You can save time by making the vinaigrette in the bottom of the salad serving bowl, then adding the mushrooms—which thus get the benefit of a marinade—and piling the greens on top. But do not toss the salad until you are just ready to serve.

The rich sauce of this menu needs a full-bodied wine. Perla Meyers suggests the berry flavor of a California zinfandel, an unusual pairing of red wine and chicken. Alternatively, you might try an imported brut rosé Champagne.

SHOPPING LIST AND STAPLES

4 Rock Cornish game hens
8 medium-size white turnips
1 head Boston lettuce
¼ pound fresh spinach
6 large fresh mushrooms
2 heads garlic (about 18 large cloves)
1 bunch fresh parsley
2 tablespoons chopped fresh dill, or 2 teaspoons dried
1 lemon
1 cup heavy cream
6 tablespoons butter
1 teaspoon green peppercorns
2 cups chicken broth
6 tablespoons olive oil
1 teaspoon vegetable oil
¼ cup sherry wine vinegar or red wine vinegar
1 tablespoon flour
4 teaspoons sugar
2½ tablespoons dark brown sugar
1 tablespoon chopped fresh thyme, or 1 teaspoon dried
1½ teaspoons chopped fresh rosemary, or
    ½ teaspoon dried
1 teaspoon paprika
2 tablespoons Dijon mustard
Coarse (kosher) salt
White pepper
Salt and pepper

UTENSILS

2 large heavy skillets with covers, one with
    oven-proof handle
Small saucepan
Salad bowl
2 small bowls
Measuring cups and spoons
Chef's knife
Slotted spoon

Tongs
Whisk
Trussing string
Vegetable peeler
Poultry shears
Juicer

START-TO-FINISH STEPS

1. Follow game hen recipe step 1.
2. Chop herbs for game hen and salad recipes.
3. Follow game hen recipe steps 2 through 5.
4. Juice lemon and follow salad recipe steps 1 through 3.
5. Follow turnip recipe steps 1 through 4. Keep warm.
6. Follow game hen recipe steps 6 through 11.
7. Follow salad recipe step 4 and serve with game hens and turnips.

RECIPES

Game Hens with Green Peppercorn Sauce

18 large cloves garlic
1 tablespoon Dijon mustard
1 teaspoon paprika
1 tablespoon chopped fresh thyme, or 1 teaspoon dried
1½ teaspoons chopped fresh rosemary, or
   ½ teaspoon dried
4 Rock Cornish game hens
Coarse (kosher) salt and freshly ground black pepper
3 tablespoons butter
1 teaspoon vegetable oil
1½ cups chicken broth
1 tablespoon flour
1 cup heavy cream
1 heaping teaspoon green peppercorns, crushed
Parsley sprigs for garnish (optional)

1. Preheat oven to 400 degrees.

2. Mash 2 of the garlic cloves. Combine in small bowl with mustard, paprika, thyme, and rosemary. Blend mixture into a paste and rub hens well with it. Season hens with coarse salt and freshly ground black pepper. Truss hens (see diagrams at right).

3. In skillet with oven-proof handle, heat 2 tablespoons of the butter and oil until foam subsides. Add game hens and sauté over moderate heat on both sides until they are lightly browned.

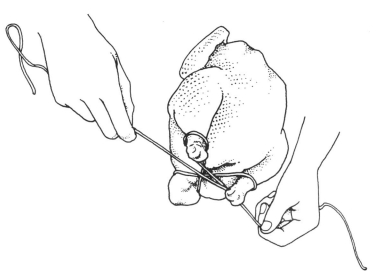

Tuck tips of wings under back securely. Tie legs and tail together, crossing string over cavity and pulling tight.

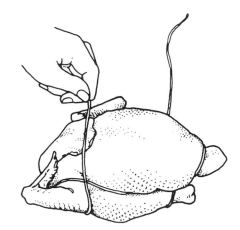

Run string under legs; turn game hen over, run string through wings. Tie securely in back, with knot over skin flap.

4. Meanwhile, bring about 1 cup water to a boil. Add the remaining 16 cloves garlic and blanch 1 to 2 minutes. Drain and slip skins off. Scatter garlic around hens and add half of the broth. Place uncovered in oven.

5. Baste hens every 10 minutes with the remaining chicken broth. Turn them once during their cooking time and make sure pan juices are not burning.

6. Cook 30 to 35 minutes, or until tender. Remove hens and set them aside. With slotted spoon, remove garlic

cloves and reserve.

7. Skim surface of pan juices of any fat. Place pan over high heat and reduce liquid by half.

8. Combine flour with the remaining 1 tablespoon butter and work together with your fingers until thoroughly blended, making *beurre manié*.

9. Add cream to reduced sauce. Taste and season with salt and pepper. Whisk in a little of the *beurre manié*, just enough for sauce to thicken. Taste and correct seasoning.

10. Return garlic cloves to skillet. Add crushed green peppercorns and heat sauce through. Keep warm.

11. Remove trussing string, and quarter game hens with poultry shears. Place on serving platter and spoon sauce over them. Garnish with sprigs of parsley, if desired.

Sweet and Sour Turnips

8 medium-size white turnips
3 tablespoons butter
Salt and freshly ground white pepper
1 teaspoon sugar
½ cup chicken broth
2½ heaping tablespoons dark brown sugar
¼ cup sherry wine vinegar or red wine vinegar

1. Peel turnips. Cut them crosswise into ¾-inch slices and then into ¾-inch cubes.

2. In skillet, melt butter. Add turnips. Season with salt, white pepper, and sugar. Cook turnips over medium-low heat, tossing them in pan until they are glazed and nicely browned. Lower heat and add a little of the chicken broth. Cover pan and cook 15 minutes. You may need to add a little more of the broth. Do not over cook.

3. While turnips are cooking, combine brown sugar with vinegar in small bowl. Blend well and add to turnips after they have cooked 15 minutes.

4. Raise heat and cook until turnips are well glazed and pan juices are reduced to about 2 tablespoons. Remove to serving dish and pour pan juices over them.

Green Salad with Lemon Mustard Vinaigrette

¼ pound fresh spinach
1 head Boston lettuce
6 large fresh mushrooms
Juice of 1 lemon
1 tablespoon Dijon mustard
3 teaspoons sugar
Freshly ground black pepper
2 tablespoons chopped fresh dill, or 2 teaspoons dried
6 tablespoons olive oil

1. Trim stems from spinach. Wash and dry spinach and lettuce. Slice mushrooms.

2. In bottom of salad bowl, whisk lemon juice, mustard, sugar, pepper, dill, and olive oil together. Vinaigrette will be very thick.

3. Add sliced mushrooms to vinaigrette and toss to coat them. Add lettuce and spinach to salad bowl. Refrigerate until serving time.

4. Toss salad and serve.

ADDED TOUCHES

For a variation on the turnip recipe, use six small turnips instead of eight, but add two or three carrots, each cut into strips about an inch long. Then proceed with the recipe.

If you have time, prepare the following dessert before you begin to cook dinner. Complete the recipe but leave the pears and sauce in the skillet and let them cool. Reheat just before serving, being careful not to let the cream boil.

Sautéed Pears in Caramel Cream

4 large semiripe pears
2 tablespoons butter
½ cup plus 1 tablespoon sugar
¾ cup heavy cream
2 tablespoons water
Pinch of freshly grated nutmeg
1 pint vanilla ice cream (optional)

1. Peel pears, cut in half, core, and cut ⅛-inch-deep scores. Reserve.

2. In 10-inch heavy iron skillet, heat butter. Add pears and sauté over fairly high heat until lightly browned. Add 1 tablespoon of the sugar and continue sautéing pears until soft and caramelized, or about 4 to 5 minutes.

3. While pears are sautéing, heat cream in small saucepan and reserve.

4. In 2-quart heavy saucepan heat sugar and water. Cook sugar until it turns deep caramel color. Remove from heat and add hot cream. Whisk mixture until cream and caramel are well blended and sauce is smooth. Add pinch of nutmeg, and when pears are done, add cream to skillet and mix into pears. Transfer pears to serving plates and serve with a side dish of vanilla ice cream, if desired.

Shirley Sarvis

I f there were an official California style in American cooking, the simplicity of Shirley Sarvis's approach would define it. A California-based author and food consultant, she puts a high value on fresh ingredients and believes that the flavor of one dish should not overwhelm that of the next.

Quick cooking techniques are very much a part of her ideas, and she devised Menu 1 for the cook in a hurry who nevertheless wants the elegance and appeal of a whole, roasted chicken, which traditionally has been the focal point of big company dinners. Use a small fryer, not more than two and a half pounds; it roasts in about 45 minutes, requires little basting, and tastes as good as any roaster two or three times as large. Accompanied by garlic-flavored, grated zucchini and a first course of French bread and cheese, this will serve four nicely.

In the baked chicken breasts in Menu 2, nutmeg—a spice you may not often have tried in main-course dishes—flavors the brandy sauce. Nutmeg also appears in the spinach in Menu 3. Buy nutmeg whole and grate what you need as you cook—a bit of extra work, perhaps, but well worth the effort for the flavor and the aroma.

Finding the right wine for a Shirley Sarvis menu might sound tricky, especially when the recipes include—as does Menu 1—goat cheese, garlic-accented vegetables, and lemon-flavored chicken. A dry white wine is generally best; specific suggestions are listed with the recipes.

A bright cloth, a small bowl of cut flowers, and an oval platter make an appealing setting for this lemon-roasted chicken, stir-fried zucchini, and French bread garnished with goat cheese and black olives. Pass the bread basket around the table and ask a guest to pour the wine while you return briefly to the kitchen to disjoint the chicken.

Cheese and French Bread
Lemon-Roasted Chicken
Shredded Zucchini with Garlic

The juice from the easy stuffing of lemon slices in this small, fast-roasting chicken flavors the bird during the cooking, and the lemon slices do not add to the cooking time, as would a solid stuffing.

For maximum flavor from a two- to two-and-a-half-pound bird, buy a fresh, not a frozen, chicken and cook it the same day you buy it. Bring it to room temperature before you roast it: a cold chicken takes longer to cook. Roast the bird untrussed. This not only saves preparation time, but allows the leg meat to be done at the same time as the breast.

Although the two-and-a-half-pound bird will serve four, you may want to roast two broiler-fryers at the same time in order to offer second helpings and to make leftovers for salads or sandwiches the next day.

Testing with an instant-reading meat thermometer is the best way to tell if the chicken is done. Insert the point in the thickest part of the thigh just before the 45 minutes are up. Experienced chefs do not recommend the kind of meat thermometer that stays in the bird while it cooks. These simply create an escape path for the juices and at the same time conduct heat too rapidly to the interior of the bird. Another test: move the drumstick. The joint should feel loose.

Zucchini, the dark-green member of the summer squash family, peaks during the summer but is available—and is often good—in other seasons. Select medium-size specimens with a good deep color and unblemished skins. Avoid very large zucchini, which tend to be bland and seedy. Zucchini keep a week or more in the refrigerator, so you can shop ahead for them.

WHAT TO DRINK

Simplicity is the keynote of this meal, and the best choices for wine would be a California Sauvignon Blanc (or Fumé Blanc), a French Pouilly-Fumé, or a Sancerre: all made from the Sauvignon Blanc grape, but endowed with different flavors by varying soil and climate conditions.

SHOPPING LIST AND STAPLES

2½-pound broiler-fryer chicken
2 lemons
6 to 8 medium-size zucchini (about 2 pounds)
2 cloves garlic
8 tablespoons butter (1 stick)

½ pound fresh young goat cheese, such as Montrachet, Boucheron, or Sainte Maure
½ pound Greek olives (optional)
1 loaf French bread
Salt
Freshly ground black pepper

UTENSILS

Food processor or grater
2 large heavy skillets, one with oven-proof handle
Measuring spoons
All-purpose knife
Bread knife
Wooden spatula
Instant-reading meat thermometer
2 small metal skewers
Poultry shears

START-TO-FINISH STEPS

1. Follow chicken recipe steps 1 through 3.
2. Follow zucchini recipe steps 1 through 3.
3. Follow chicken recipe step 4.
4. Slice additional lemon for garnish, if desired, and set aside. Mince garlic for zucchini recipe.
5. Follow cheese and French bread recipe steps 1 and 2.
6. Follow chicken recipe step 5.
7. Follow zucchini recipe steps 4 through 7.
8. Follow chicken recipe steps 6 and 7. Serve with zucchini.

RECIPES

Cheese and French Bread

1 loaf French bread
½ pound fresh young goat cheese, such as Montrachet, Boucheron, or Sainte Maure
½ pound Greek olives for garnish (optional)

1. With bread knife, cut bread into thick slices.
2. Arrange bread and cheese on serving platter. Garnish with olives, if desired. Serve as first course.

Lemon-Roasted Chicken

2½-pound broiler-fryer chicken, at room temperature

Salt and freshly ground black pepper
2 lemons

1. Preheat oven to 400 degrees.
2. Remove any excess fat from chicken. Rub chicken inside and out very generously with salt and pepper. Cut 1 of the lemons into 12 slices and place in cavity of bird. Close neck and tail cavities with small skewers. Tuck wings under body of bird.
3. Place chicken, breast side down, in well-oiled skillet with oven-proof handle. Roast in oven 15 minutes.
4. With aid of spatula, lift chicken carefully and turn it breast side up. Try not to tear skin. Roast about 35 minutes more.
5. Test for doneness. Transfer to platter and let chicken rest in warm place 5 minutes. Remove skewers.
6. Add pan juices to drippings in skillet; heat and stir to blend. Spoon over chicken or serve separately. Garnish chicken with fresh slices of remaining lemon, if desired.
7. When ready to serve, disjoint chicken.

Shredded Zucchini with Garlic

6 to 8 medium-size zucchini (about 2 pounds)
8 tablespoons butter (1 stick)
2 cloves garlic, minced
1 teaspoon salt

1. Trim off zucchini ends, but do not peel.
2. Shred zucchini using grater or food processor.
3. Wrap grated zucchini in clean dish towel and squeeze out as much moisture as possible.
4. Heat butter in skillet over medium-high heat until it bubbles.
5. Add zucchini, garlic, and salt.
6. Sauté about 2 minutes, turning with spatula, until zucchini is heated through, barely tender, and still crisp.
7. Remove zucchini to serving dish and keep warm.

ADDED TOUCHES

If you have extra time, here are two fruit desserts that will go well with the lemon chicken or with either of the other two Shirley Sarvis menus. Baked apple slices with apricots is an unusual variation on the venerable American favorite, apple crisp. The apricots will overwhelm a bland apple, so be sure to select tart ones. Jonathans, Winesaps, or Granny Smiths would be good choices.

The plum-port compote will look especially interesting if you use two varieties of plum. The compote makes a fine sauce for vanilla ice cream, also.

Baked Apple Slices with Apricots

3 ounces (½ cup firmly packed) dried apricots
1 pound tart cooking apples
2 teaspoons lemon juice
½ cup sugar
Pinch of ground cinnamon
3 tablespoons finely chopped blanched almonds
4 tablespoons butter, melted
¼ teaspoon vanilla

1. Cover apricots with boiling water and let stand 15 minutes. Drain well.
2. Preheat oven to 425 degrees.
3. Peel, quarter, and core apples. Cut into ¼-inch crosswise slices and put in bowl. Add lemon juice and 1 tablespoon of the sugar and mix gently.
4. Butter 3-cup soufflé dish.
5. Spread half of the apples in soufflé dish. Top with layer of apricots and then the remaining apples.
6. Stir together the remaining sugar, cinnamon, almonds, butter, and vanilla and sprinkle over apples.
7. Bake until topping is browned and apples are tender, about 30 minutes. If necessary, cover top loosely with foil during last 5 minutes of baking to prevent over browning.
8. Place on rack to cool until just warm.

Plum-Port Compote

Zest from ½ orange
1 pound fresh red or purple plums
⅓ cup sugar
⅓ cup ruby port
½ cup water
½ vanilla bean, split and some seeds scraped loose
1½ teaspoons fresh lemon juice

1. Cut zest into thinnest possible strips.
2. Halve and pit plums.
3. Combine zest, sugar, port, water, vanilla bean with seeds, and lemon juice in saucepan. Heat to boiling, stirring to dissolve sugar.
4. Add plums and simmer just until barely tender, 3 to 10 minutes depending on size. Cover saucepan if plums are large and firm.
5. As plums are tender, lift them out with slotted spoon and arrange in single layer in shallow serving bowl.
6. Pour cooking syrup over plums and chill.

Ham and French Bread
Baked Chicken Breasts with Brandy Sauce
Green Beans / Boston Lettuce Salad

Offer the French bread and ham as an hors d'oeuvre with a glass of wine. That will give you time to finish the brandy sauce for the chicken breasts and toss the green beans in butter and the salad in the vinaigrette.

Cooking boned chicken breasts is an exact science. They are done as soon as they turn from pink to white in the thickest part, and over cooking will toughen them. The best way to test is by touch. If they feel springy to the pad of your index finger, they are done. In this menu, the halved breasts spend only about 15 minutes in the oven and, in fact, should be slightly underdone when you remove them, since they will continue to cook in their own heat.

The brandy sauce for the chicken is an unusual blend of good things: wine, brandy, tarragon, mustard, nutmeg, and cream. Too often treated as merely an ingredient for spice cakes and eggnog, nutmeg was for centuries a favorite seasoning for meats and deserves to return to its former eminence.

WHAT TO DRINK

Many white wines would nicely accompany this dish. You might serve a New York or California Chardonnay, which is full-bodied; an Alsatian Riesling, spicy and aromatic; or an Italian Verdicchio, crisp and clean tasting.

SHOPPING LIST AND STAPLES

4 unskinned boneless chicken breast halves
¼ pound Bayonne or Black Forest ham, thinly sliced
1 pound fresh green beans
2 heads Boston lettuce
1 bunch watercress (optional)
2 teaspoons minced fresh tarragon, or ½ teaspoon dried
Tarragon sprigs (optional)
4 tablespoons butter
¼ cup heavy cream
½ cup chicken broth
1 loaf French bread
¼ cup olive oil
2 teaspoons red wine vinegar
½ teaspoon Dijon mustard
⅛ teaspoon paprika
Whole nutmeg
Salt and pepper
1 cup dry white wine
¼ cup brandy

UTENSILS

Large heavy skillet with oven-proof handle

Large saucepan with cover
2 small bowls
Colander
Measuring cups and spoons
Bread knife
Nutmeg grater
Whisk

START-TO-FINISH STEPS

1. Follow chicken recipe step 1.
2. Follow salad recipe steps 1 and 2.
3. Follow bean recipe steps 1 and 2.
4. Follow chicken recipe steps 2 through 4. As chicken bakes, follow bean recipe step 3.
5. Follow chicken recipe step 5, grate nutmeg, and follow chicken recipe step 6.
6. Follow ham and French bread recipe steps 1 and 2.
7. Follow salad recipe step 3.
8. Follow bean recipe step 4.
9. Follow chicken recipe step 7.
10. Serve beans, salad, and chicken.

RECIPES

Ham and French Bread

¼ pound Bayonne or Black Forest ham, thinly sliced
1 loaf French bread

1. Arrange ham on serving platter.
2. Cut bread into thick slices, and place on platter with ham. Serve as first course.

Baked Chicken Breasts with Brandy Sauce

3 tablespoons butter
4 unskinned boneless chicken breast halves
½ teaspoon salt
Freshly ground black pepper
1 cup dry white wine
½ cup chicken broth
¼ cup brandy
¼ cup heavy cream
2 teaspoons minced fresh tarragon, or ½ teaspoon dried
½ teaspoon Dijon mustard
⅛ teaspoon paprika
Pinch of freshly grated nutmeg

Fresh tarragon sprigs or watercress
  for garnish (optional)

1. Preheat oven to 425 degrees.
2. Melt butter in skillet. Coat each breast piece by turning it in melted butter. Season with salt and pepper.
3. Pull skin neatly under edges of breast halves, each forming a compact shape about 1½ inches thick. Arrange them, skin side up, in skillet.
4. Bake chicken breasts 15 minutes, or until done, basting occasionally with pan drippings. Remove them to serving platter and keep warm.
5. Add wine, chicken broth, and brandy to skillet. Cook over high heat, stirring, until liquid is reduced to about ½ cup.
6. In small bowl, mix together cream, tarragon, mustard, paprika, and nutmeg. Add mixture to skillet and cook, stirring, until sauce is reduced and thickened.
7. Spoon sauce over breasts and garnish with tarragon sprigs or watercress, if desired.

Buttered Green Beans

1 pound fresh green beans
Salt
1 tablespoon butter

1. Bring large saucepan of water to a boil.
2. Trim ends of beans and rinse.
3. When water boils, add salt and beans. Simmer uncovered until beans are just tender, 8 to 10 minutes. Drain well and cover pan to keep warm.
4. Just before serving, gently toss with butter and season to taste.

Boston Lettuce Salad

2 heads Boston lettuce
¼ cup olive oil
2 teaspoons red wine vinegar
⅛ teaspoon salt
Freshly ground black pepper

1. Rinse and dry lettuce leaves. Break lettuce into large bite-size pieces and chill.
2. Whisk together oil, vinegar, and salt in bowl.
3. Just before serving, toss lettuce with only enough dressing to lightly coat leaves. Add freshly ground black pepper to taste.

Poached Chicken with Parsley Butter Sauce
Steamed Fresh Spinach
Rice

Relatively simple, and thus an excellent family meal for midweek, chicken combines with parsley butter sauce, rice, and spinach.

Fresh parsley, which often sits uneaten at the side of a serving plate, is rich in vitamin A and ounce for ounce has more iron than spinach, and more vitamin C than an orange. In this menu, it is a major ingredient in the sauce for poached chicken. Buy fresh parsley; avoid bunches with yellow spots, which indicate age. (Do not use dried parsley: it is flavorless and lacks all food value.) Trim the stems, wash the leaves under running water, and shake the bunch dry. Stored in plastic, it will keep in the refrigerator for a week. Add a piece of paper towel to absorb the moisture; or make a bouquet of the parsley in a glass of water, cover the glass with a plastic bag, and refrigerate it in some far corner (so you do not knock it over when reaching for the milk).

Steamed spinach takes on an interesting taste when cooked with a chili pepper, as Shirley Sarvis recommends here. Do not serve the red pepper, which is too fiery to eat with this meal but does make an attractive garnish.

WHAT TO DRINK

A fruity white wine, preferably an Alsatian Riesling, is the cook's first choice. Hot tea served plain in Chinese cups would also be appropriate.

3-pound broiler-fryer chicken, cut into serving pieces
1 stalk celery with leaves
1 small onion
2 pounds fresh spinach
1 bunch fresh parsley
1 dried hot red pepper
1 lemon
11 tablespoons butter (1 stick plus 3 tablespoons)
2 eggs
1 cup short- or long-grain white rice
Whole nutmeg
Pinch of sugar
Salt and pepper

UTENSILS

Heavy casserole with cover
Steamer or large saucepan with cover
Medium-size heavy saucepan with cover
Small saucepan
Colander
Measuring cups and spoons
All-purpose knife
Slotted spoon
Nutmeg grater
Juicer

START-TO-FINISH STEPS

In the morning: follow parsley butter sauce recipe step 1.
1. Chop onion for chicken recipe, and parsley for parsley butter sauce recipe.
2. Follow chicken recipe steps 1 and 2. As chicken simmers, follow spinach recipe step 1.
3. Follow rice recipe steps 1 and 2. With rice and chicken simmering, grate nutmeg and follow spinach recipe steps 2 and 3.
4. Juice lemon and follow parsley butter recipe steps 2 through 5.
5. Follow spinach recipe step 4.
6. Follow chicken recipe steps 3 and 4 and serve with rice and spinach.

RECIPES

Poached Chicken

3-pound broiler-fryer chicken, cut into serving pieces
1 stalk celery with leaves
1 small onion, quartered
1 large parsley sprig
1½ teaspoons salt
Freshly ground black pepper
Parsley sprigs for garnish (optional)
Parsley butter sauce (see following recipe)

1. Place chicken, celery, onion, sprig of parsley, salt, and pepper in casserole. Add cold water to cover.

2. Bring water to a boil. Reduce heat, cover casserole, and simmer about 45 minutes, or until chicken is tender.
3. With slotted spoon, transfer chicken pieces to warm serving plates or platter. Garnish with sprigs of parsley, if desired.
4. Serve with parsley butter sauce.

Parsley Butter Sauce

2 eggs
11 tablespoons butter (1 stick plus 3 tablespoons)
¼ teaspoon salt
Freshly ground black pepper
4 teaspoons lemon juice
⅔ cup finely chopped parsley

1. Put eggs into small saucepan and cover with cold water. Heat to boiling, then simmer 12 to 14 minutes. Drain, cool, and peel under cold running water; dry and chill.
2. When eggs are cool, finely chop them.
3. In small saucepan, melt butter over low heat. Stir in salt, pepper, lemon juice, parsley, and chopped eggs.
4. Heat sauce just enough to warm it through. Serve garnished with parsley sprigs, if desired.

Steamed Fresh Spinach

2 pounds fresh spinach
1 dried hot red pepper
Pinch of freshly grated nutmeg
Pinch of sugar
Pinch of salt
Freshly ground black pepper

1. Remove any coarse stems from spinach leaves. Wash leaves well in 2 or 3 changes of cold water. Do not dry.
2. Put wet leaves in vegetable steamer or saucepan with tight-fitting cover. Add hot red pepper, nutmeg, sugar, salt, and pepper.
3. Cover and cook about 5 minutes, turning occasionally, until spinach is just tender.
4. Drain spinach well in colander or strainer. Discard red pepper or use it as a garnish.

Rice

2 cups lightly salted water
1 cup short- or long-grain white rice

1. Bring water to a boil. Add rice and cover tightly. Reduce heat to low.
2. Simmer about 20 minutes, or until rice is tender and all water absorbed. Fluff with fork.

ADDED TOUCH

Toasted almonds, whole and unblanched, are an appropriate garnish for the chicken, rice, and spinach. Spread about three-fourths of a cup on a baking sheet and toast in a 400-degree oven for five minutes. You can also toast them in a heavy skillet over low heat, stirring constantly, for about two minutes. Pass the almonds at the table.

Mary Beth Clark

One of the oldest and most useful tricks in cooking chicken breasts is to stuff them under the skin. You can use a wide variety of stuffings — ground meats, rice, or cheese. Not only will these add different flavors to the chicken, but they also keep the breast meat moist as it cooks. And the results can be as beautiful to look at as they are appetizing—a valuable addition to your repertoire of company dinners and a boost to your reputation as a good cook.

The three menus that Mary Beth Clark creates here offer variations on this theme. In Menu 1, she stuffs the chicken breasts with a savory homemade pâté and finishes them with a Cognac sauce. In Menu 2, the stuffing is a mild but delicious combination of Parmesan and ricotta cheese. The third variation is chicken breasts with Persian rice, an unusual mixture of rice, fruit, and nuts topped off with an orange-flavored sauce. The vegetables include asparagus and baby carrots—familiar on every table—as well as such relative newcomers to American menus as celeriac—a turniplike root—and sugar snap peas.

Boneless—but unskinned—chicken breasts stuffed with your own mixture of ground veal, pork, and prosciutto make an impressive main course for an important small dinner. Slice the breasts about a half inch thick and serve them on a platter garnished with celeriac puree. As you serve each plate at the table, spoon the creamy Cognac sauce onto each slice. The watercress salad should have a separate plate; you may wish to serve it as a second course.

46

Chicken Breasts Stuffed with Pâté in Sauce Suprême
Celeriac Puree
Watercress Salad

Celeriac, a standard vegetable on French menus, is a type of celery with a knobby and edible root that has only recently begun to appear in American markets and on American tables. Blanched, diced, and dressed with a mustard mayonnaise, it becomes *céleri rémoulade*, a popular appetizer or buffet dish. Brown celeriac root looks so unprepossessing that you may not have noticed it in the produce department, but most large supermarkets now stock it in the fall and winter. Buy firm, small to medium-size knobs and refrigerate until you are ready to peel and cook them; they will keep from one to two weeks.

If you do not wish to bone the chicken breasts yourself, you will probably have to get them from a butcher, since you need to have boneless breasts with the skin left on. Spicy, cured ham will do fine as a substitute for the prosciutto, which tends to be costly.

Watercress, which belongs to the nasturtium family, has long stems and small, spicy leaves—and is very good alone, as in this recipe, or when mixed with other greens. A good produce market will usually keep it on crushed ice. Store watercress in plastic in the coldest part of the refrigerator. It should keep three or four days. Wash it just before using.

Sherry wine vinegar, one ingredient of the salad dressing, is a comparatively new item in American kitchens. Imported from Spain, as are the finest sherries, this vinegar is rich, sweet, and fairly expensive. Moreover, you may have to shop for it in a specialty shop or gourmet store. If you cannot find sherry vinegar, then you should substitute a good red wine vinegar.

WHAT TO DRINK

This special dish calls for a white Burgundy—a Meursault or, for a really festive occasion, a Montrachet. A less expensive alternative is to serve a lightly chilled Beaujolais, which would go well with these robust flavors.

SHOPPING LIST AND STAPLES

2 whole unskinned boneless chicken breasts
6 ounces ground pork
4 ounces ground veal
2 ounces prosciutto
2 bunches watercress
2 to 3 knobs celeriac (about 2 pounds)

3 large shallots
1 clove garlic
1 bunch fresh parsley
1 teaspoon minced fresh thyme, or ½ teaspoon dried
1 lemon
2 teaspoons unsalted butter
10 tablespoons salted butter (1¼ sticks)
½ cup heavy cream
1 egg
½ cup chicken broth
4 ounces shelled walnuts
3 tablespoons plus 2 teaspoons olive oil
1 tablespoon sunflower oil
2½ teaspoons red wine vinegar
2 teaspoons sherry wine vinegar
Pinch of ground allspice
Whole nutmeg
White pepper
Salt and pepper
¼ cup plus 2 teaspoons brandy or Cognac

UTENSILS

Food processor or food mill
Vegetable steamer
Large skillet
Medium-size saucepan
Shallow baking pan
Cookie sheet
Large bowl
Small bowl
Measuring cups and spoons
Chef's knife
All-purpose knife
2 wooden spatulas
Nutmeg grater
Cake rack
Juicer
Whisk
Instant-reading meat thermometer
Metal skewers (optional)

START-TO-FINISH STEPS

1. Follow watercress salad recipe steps 1 through 4.
2. Mince shallots, prosciutto, parsley, garlic, and thyme for chicken recipe. Grate nutmeg for celeriac and sauce

suprême recipes. Juice lemon for sauce suprême.
3. Follow chicken recipe steps 1 through 6.
4. Follow celeriac recipe step 1.
5. Follow chicken recipe steps 7 through 11. As chicken roasts, follow celeriac recipe steps 2 and 3, and then follow chicken recipe step 12.
6. Follow salad recipe step 5.
7. Follow celeriac recipe step 4.
8. Follow chicken recipe step 13.
9. Serve chicken with puree and salad.

RECIPES

Chicken Breasts Stuffed with Pâté

The stuffing:
6 ounces ground pork
4 ounces ground veal
2 ounces prosciutto, minced
3 tablespoons minced shallots
1 tablespoon finely chopped fresh parsley
¼ teaspoon minced garlic
2 teaspoons brandy or Cognac
Pinch of ground allspice
1 teaspoon minced fresh thyme, or ½ teaspoon dried
⅓ teaspoon salt
Freshly ground white pepper
1 large egg, well beaten

The chicken:
2 whole unskinned boneless chicken breasts
2 teaspoons unsalted butter
2 teaspoons olive oil
Sauce suprême (see following recipe)

1. In large bowl, combine all ingredients for pâté stuffing. Mix ingredients well, cover, and let flavors blend.
2. With knife, trim and discard fat, sinew, and cartilage from chicken breasts, keeping skin intact.
3. To form pockets for stuffing, gently separate skin from flesh with your fingers where breastbone was, keeping skin and flesh intact around remaining edges. If necessary, use knife to cut out tissue where skin and meat are attached along center of each breast.
4. Fill pockets with pâté mixture.
5. Smooth skin over filling so it is completely covered, and pull skin down around filling, tucking all edges under flesh of breasts. Use metal skewers, if necessary, to keep skins attached.
6. Turn oven to 375 degrees.
7. Heat oil in large skillet and add butter.
8. Place breasts, stuffed side up, in skillet and sear over high heat 2 to 3 minutes. Turn, and sear 1 to 2 minutes more.
9. Holding each breast between 2 spatulas, tilt, and sear any raw edges.
10. Over moderate heat, sauté, stuffed side up, for additional 2 minutes.
11. Remove pan from heat. Transfer chicken to cake rack set on baking pan. Roast 18 to 22 minutes, or until meat thermometer registers 155° degrees. Turn off oven and leave breasts in it.
12. Drain off any fat from skillet and make sauce suprême.
13. Remove skewers, if used, and cut each breast into ½-inch slices. Spoon sauce over each portion.

Sauce Suprême

¼ cup brandy or Cognac
½ cup chicken broth
½ cup heavy cream
1½ teaspoons lemon juice
Salt and freshly ground white pepper
Freshly grated nutmeg
2 tablespoons frozen, salted butter

1. Place skillet used for sautéing breasts over high heat and add brandy. Deglaze pan by stirring and scraping bottom until liquid is reduced by half.
2. Turn heat to moderate, add broth and heavy cream, and cook—stirring—until reduced by half.
3. Add lemon juice and season with salt, white pepper, and nutmeg. Remove from heat and whisk in butter.

Celeriac Puree

2 to 3 knobs celeriac (about 2 pounds)
8 tablespoons salted butter (1 stick)
Salt and freshly ground white pepper
Freshly grated nutmeg
4 tablespoons finely chopped fresh parsley

1. Peel celeriac and cut into ½-inch slices. Place in vegetable steamer and steam over boiling water about 10 minutes, or until tender.
2. Chop steamed celeriac coarsely and puree it in food processor or food mill.
3. Melt butter and stir in puree. Add salt, white pepper, and nutmeg to taste. When heated through, cover and keep warm until serving time.
4. Sprinkle 1 tablespoon fresh parsley over each serving.

Watercress Salad

2 bunches watercress
4 ounces shelled walnuts
3 tablespoons olive oil
1 tablespoon sunflower oil
4½ teaspoons wine vinegar, preferably 2½ teaspoons red wine vinegar and 2 teaspoons sherry wine vinegar
Salt and freshly ground black pepper

1. Preheat oven to 350 degrees.
2. Wash watercress and dry thoroughly. Remove any tough stems. Refrigerate until serving time.
3. Toast walnuts on cookie sheet in oven about 5 minutes. Set aside until cool; then chop them.
4. In small bowl, mix together oils and vinegars with small whisk. Season to taste.
5. At serving time, toss watercress with vinaigrette and sprinkle toasted walnuts on top.

Chicken Breasts Stuffed with Cheese
Steamed Asparagus with Tarragon Butter

Stuffed chicken breasts make a perfect light weekend lunch. Fresh asparagus is a perfect accompaniment.

Ricotta (the word means "buttermilk curd"), the cheese for the stuffing in this chicken menu, is a close Italian cousin of cottage cheese but slightly sweeter. You can buy ricotta fresh from the kitchen in Italian markets or prepackaged at the supermarket.

Two savory herbs—marjoram and thyme—flavor this cheese stuffing. Both are part of the mint family, and both are easy to grow in a sunny window box.

Tarragon, the herb for the asparagus, is better fresh but acceptable dried. Its sharp aroma and licorice flavor give it many uses. Employ it judiciously. Too much of it will overpower asparagus.

WHAT TO DRINK

A crisp wine, either a California Fumé Blanc or a French Pouilly-Fumé, should accompany this meal. Both have a hint of smokiness to add to the flavors' harmony.

SHOPPING LIST AND STAPLES

2 whole unskinned boneless chicken breasts
1½ to 2 pounds fresh asparagus
2 medium-size yellow onions
2 cloves garlic

1½ tablespoons minced fresh marjoram,
    or 1½ teaspoons dried
2 teaspoons minced fresh thyme, or ½ teaspoon dried
3 tablespoons minced fresh tarragon, or
    3 teaspoons dried
2 medium-size lemons
¼ pound Parmesan cheese
⅓ cup ricotta cheese
8 tablespoons (1 stick) plus 2 teaspoons butter
1 large egg
2 teaspoons olive oil
Whole nutmeg
White pepper
Salt

UTENSILS

Large skillet
Broiler pan
Vegetable steamer
2 small saucepans
2 bowls
Measuring cups and spoons
Chef's knife
All-purpose knife
2 wooden spatulas
Nutmeg grater
Metal skewers (optional)
Vegetable peeler

START-TO-FINISH STEPS

1. Chop onion and garlic, julienne lemon peel, grate nutmeg, and Parmesan cheese, and mince herbs for chicken recipe. Mince tarragon for asparagus recipe.
2. Follow chicken recipe steps 1 through 12.
3. Follow asparagus recipe steps 1 and 2.
4. Follow chicken recipe steps 13 through 15.
5. Follow asparagus recipe step 3.
6. Serve chicken and asparagus.

RECIPES

Chicken Breasts Stuffed with Cheese

The stuffing:
2 tablespoons butter
¾ cup chopped onions
2 teaspoons minced garlic
Peel of 2 medium-size lemons, finely julienned
⅓ cup ricotta cheese
2 tablespoons freshly grated Parmesan cheese
1½ tablespoons minced fresh marjoram,
    or 1½ teaspoons dried
2 teaspoons minced fresh thyme, or ½ teaspoon dried
Freshly ground white pepper
Salt
Freshly grated nutmeg
1 egg yolk from large egg

The chicken:
2 whole unskinned boneless chicken breasts
2 teaspoons butter
2 teaspoons olive oil
4 tablespoons freshly grated Parmesan cheese

1. In saucepan, melt butter and sauté onion until soft but not brown.
2. Add garlic and lemon peel and mix quickly. Transfer to bowl and cool.
3. Put ricotta cheese, 2 tablespoons Parmesan cheese, herbs, and seasonings in another bowl and mix well. Add egg yolk and garlic mixture and mix until well blended. Cover and refrigerate.
4. With sharp knife, trim and discard fat, sinew, and cartilage from chicken breasts, keeping skin intact.
5. To form pockets for stuffing, gently separate skin from flesh with your fingers where breastbone was, keeping skin and flesh intact around remaining edges. If necessary, use knife to cut out tissue where skin and meat are attached along center of each breast.
6. Fill pockets with cheese stuffing.
7. Smooth skin over filling so it is completely covered, and pull skin down around filling, tucking all edges under flesh of breasts. Use metal skewers, if necessary, to keep skin attached.
8. Melt butter in skillet and add oil.
9. Add breasts, stuffed side up, and sear over high heat 2 minutes. Turn and sear 1 to 2 minutes.
10. Holding each breast between 2 spatulas, tilt, and sear any raw edges.
11. Over moderate heat, sauté breasts, stuffed side up, 15 minutes.
12. Meanwhile, place broiler pan 3 inches from heat source and turn broiler on.
13. Remove skillet from heat and sprinkle Parmesan cheese on top of each chicken breast. Press cheese down with spatula.
14. Transfer to broiler and broil about 5 minutes, or until cheese topping is light golden brown.
15. To serve, remove skewers, if used, and cut each breast in half.

Steamed Asparagus with Tarragon Butter

1½ to 2 pounds fresh asparagus
6 tablespoons butter
3 tablespoons minced fresh tarragon, or
    3 teaspoons dried
Salt
Freshly ground white pepper

1. Trim by breaking off at tender point, wash, and peel asparagus spears.
2. Place asparagus in vegetable steamer and steam over boiling water 4 to 6 minutes, or until barely tender.
3. Melt butter in saucepan and add tarragon. Remove from heat. Season to taste with salt and white pepper. Spoon over steamed asparagus.

Sautéed Chicken Breasts with Persian Rice in Orange Butter Sauce
Stir-Fried Sugar Snap Peas
Steamed Baby Carrots

In the Middle East, fruit, rice, and nut mixtures signal a feast—a wedding, for example. In this menu, rice laced with raisins and pecans forms a sweet, exotic stuffing for chicken breasts. When you soak the raisins, you can substitute port for Madeira, if you wish. The tart orange butter sauce called for in this menu is particularly good with the nuts and raisins. Using frozen butter creates a creamy, satiny sauce and helps reduce the risk of the butter separating from the sauce: a technique Mary Beth Clark has used for several years.

Flowered table linens and pure white china and serving pieces complement this Persian-inspired meal. The bright-green sugar snap peas and orange baby carrots are important elements in the visual appeal of this celebratory dinner.

The fresh vegetables around this festive dish are baby carrots—available all year round and sweeter than the larger cellophane-packed variety—and sugar snap peas, which are seasonal. These crisp, sweet peas with an edible pod resemble the Chinese snow pea but are a new and native American vegetable. Since 1978, when this vegetable was introduced, it has become a garden staple second only to tomatoes in popularity. If you have a garden, plant sugar snaps. They grow in almost any soil, need no care (they do require a fence or a few poles to climb on), and bear a crop 10 weeks after you put the seed in the ground. Since they do not mind cold weather, you can plant in early spring and replant in July for the fall.

If you have no garden, you can buy sugar snaps in good produce markets in season. When you are unable to find

them, use Chinese snow peas instead. In either case, buy bright, unblemished pods—you should be able to see the peas through the thin, green skin. Use them the same day if possible and wash just before cooking. Remove the stem and string from each pod.

Shallots, which you need for the orange butter sauce, are particularly useful onions. Milder than regular onions or garlic, shallots add a special pungency and full flavor to a sauce, but never taste too oniony. They look like miniature yellow onions and cost a great deal more per pound—but a little goes a long way. Buy firm bulbs: two or three often grow out of a single base. Large ones taste just as good as small ones and are much easier to peel and chop. Store as you would a regular onion and use before they sprout.

Baby carrots usually come in a plastic bag at the produce counter. If they are very young and tender, you probably will not need to use a vegetable peeler. Simply cut off the tops and scrub the carrots with a brush under running water to peel them. For steaming, select carrots that are of uniform size so that they will cook evenly.

WHAT TO DRINK

German wines often complement Oriental dishes surprisingly well. Their delicate touch of sweetness harmonizes very pleasingly with Eastern spices. For this menu, try a good German Riesling of the Kabinett classification or, for a slightly sweeter wine, one of the Spätlese class.

For an Oriental note, omit the wine and serve hot tea instead—Lapsang Souchong, or green tea, if you can find it. Otherwise, Earl Grey is always good.

SHOPPING LIST AND STAPLES

2 whole unskinned, boneless chicken breasts
1 pound baby carrots
¾ pound sugar snap peas
7 large shallots
1 large orange
11 tablespoons unsalted butter (1 stick plus 3 tablespoons)
5 tablespoons salted butter
1 large egg
½ cup long-grain white rice
4 ounces chopped pecans
¼ cup golden raisins
2 teaspoons olive oil
1½ tablespoons white wine vinegar
Whole nutmeg
Salt and white pepper
1 tablespoon dry white wine
2 tablespoons Madeira

UTENSILS

Vegetable steamer
Large skillet
Medium-size skillet
Heavy saucepan with cover
Nonaluminum saucepan
Small saucepan
Small bowl
Measuring cups and spoons
Chef's knife
All-purpose knife
Nutmeg grater
Vegetable peeler
2 wooden spatulas
Whisk
Juicer
Metal skewers (optional)

START-TO-FINISH STEPS

In the morning: freeze butter for orange sauce recipe.
1. Follow chicken recipe steps 1 and 2. As rice simmers, mince shallots, grate nutmeg, juice orange, and julienne orange peel for orange sauce recipe. Peel carrots for carrot recipe and trim peas for pea recipe. Chop pecans and grate nutmeg for chicken recipe.
2. Follow chicken recipe steps 3 through 12.
3. Follow orange butter sauce recipe steps 1 through 3.
4. Follow carrot recipe steps 1 through 3.
5. Follow pea recipe steps 1 through 4.
6. Follow chicken recipe step 13.
7. Serve carrots and peas with chicken.

54

RECIPES

Sautéed Chicken Breasts Stuffed with Persian Rice

The stuffing:
¼ cup golden raisins
2 tablespoons Madeira
½ cup long-grain white rice
⅔ cup water
4 tablespoons butter
4 ounces chopped pecans
⅓ cup minced shallots
6 strips orange peel, finely julienned
¼ teaspoon salt
Freshly ground white pepper
Freshly grated nutmeg
1 yolk from large egg

The chicken:
2 whole unskinned boneless chicken breasts
2 teaspoons butter
2 teaspoons olive oil
Orange butter sauce (see following recipe)

1. Soak raisins in Madeira in bowl.
2. Bring rice, water, and 1 tablespoon of the butter to a boil in heavy saucepan. Stir, scraping pan so rice does not stick. Reduce heat to low, cover, and cook 20 minutes, or until rice is just tender. Stir once during this time, scraping sides of saucepan. Add 2 tablespoons additional water if rice is too hard. Remove from heat and set aside.
3. Melt 3 tablespoons of the butter in medium-size skillet. Add chopped pecans and toss until lightly browned. Add minced shallots and sauté until barely soft but not brown. Add raisins with Madeira and orange peel and stir to mix well. Remove from heat and add mixture to rice. Stir well. Season to taste with salt, white pepper, and nutmeg. Cool.
4. When mixture is cool, stir in egg yolk. Set aside, covered.
5. With knife, trim and discard fat, sinew, and cartilage from chicken breasts, keeping skin intact.
6. To form pockets for stuffing, gently separate skin from flesh with your fingers where breastbone was, keeping skin and flesh intact around remaining edges. If necessary, use knife to cut out tissue where skin and meat are attached along center of each breast. Do not split breasts.
7. Fill pockets with rice stuffing.
8. Smooth skin over rice so it is completely covered, and pull skin down around filling, tucking edges under flesh of breast. Use metal skewers, if necessary, to keep skin attached.
9. Melt butter in large skillet and add oil.
10. Add breasts, stuffed side up, and sear over high heat 2 minutes. Turn and sear 2 more minutes.
11. Holding each breast between 2 spatulas, tilt, and sear any raw edges.
12. Over moderate heat, sauté breasts, stuffed side up, 10 to 12 minutes. Turn and cook 5 minutes.

13. Remove chicken to platter. Cut each breast in half and serve with orange butter sauce.

Orange Butter Sauce

2 tablespoons minced shallots
⅓ cup orange juice
1½ tablespoons white wine vinegar
1 tablespoon dry white wine
5 tablespoons frozen, salted butter
2 strips orange peel, finely julienned
Salt and freshly ground white pepper
Freshly grated nutmeg

1. Combine shallots, orange juice, vinegar, and wine in nonaluminum saucepan. Reduce until about 2 teaspoons of liquid remain with shallots.
2. Over very low heat, carefully whisk in frozen butter, 1 tablespoon at a time, until all is melted. The sauce should look opaque. Do not overheat or butter will separate. Remove from heat.
3. Stir in julienned orange peel and season to taste with salt, white pepper, and nutmeg.

Stir-Fried Sugar Snap Peas

¾ pound sugar snap peas
3 tablespoons butter
Salt and freshly ground white pepper

1. Remove strings from sugar snap peas.
2. Melt butter over high heat in skillet.
3. Stir fry peas about 2 minutes, or until just tender. Remove from heat.
4. Season to taste with salt and white pepper.

Steamed Baby Carrots

1 pound baby carrots
3 tablespoons butter, melted
Salt and freshly ground white pepper

1. Peel carrots and bring water to a boil in steamer.
2. Steam carrots 5 to 8 minutes, or until barely tender when pierced with fork.
3. Remove to serving dish and toss with melted butter. Season to taste with salt and white pepper.

ADDED TOUCHES

If you want to serve fresh fruit for dessert, apricots—when in season—are ideal in flavor and color for this menu. When apricots are not in season, make this dried apricot mousse the afternoon or the day before you cook the chicken. It needs to be chilled for at least two hours—and it can also sit overnight.

Apricot Mousse

6 ounces dried apricots
1 cup water
1 tablespoon sugar
1 teaspoon unflavored gelatin

2 teaspoons apricot brandy (or orange brandy, such as Cointreau, Triple Sec, or Grand Marnier)
¾ cup heavy cream
2 teaspoons confectioners' sugar
½ teaspoon vanilla extract

1. Combine apricots, water, and sugar in saucepan and simmer about 15 minutes, or until apricots are tender. Remove with slotted spoon. Reserve syrup. Cool apricots.
2. Puree apricots in food processor or blender.
3. Dissolve gelatin in 1½ tablespoons of reserved apricot syrup. Add gelatin and apricot brandy to puree and mix well. Cool.
4. Whip cream until it forms soft peaks. Add confectioners' sugar and vanilla and whip until stiff peaks form.
5. Using wooden spatula, fold in whipped cream until well blended.
6. Spoon mousse into serving bowl or individual sherbet glasses and chill 2 to 24 hours.

Grapefruit-Clove Ice

For a dessert as elegant as the main dish, try this citrus ice.

4 pink grapefruits (about 1 pound each)
2 cups plus 2 tablespoons sugar
1 cup water
½ teaspoon ground cloves

1. Roll grapefruits on hard surface to prepare for juicing. Peel grapefruits without removing membranes or white bitter pith. Slice peel of 1 grapefruit into four 3 inch long strips, each about ¼ inch wide. Reserve peel. Slice grapefruits in half and squeeze juice.
2. Bring water and 2 cups of the sugar to a boil, stirring constantly until sugar is completely dissolved and syrup is clear.
3. Remove from heat, cover, and cool to room temperature. (Leftover syrup can be stored indefinitely in tightly sealed jar at room temperature.)
4. Mix grapefruit juice and ⅓ to ½ cup of the sugar syrup, according to taste. Freeze in ice cream machine according to manufacturer's instructions, or place mixture in 9-inch square metal cake pan and freeze about 2 hours, stirring twice to distribute ice crystals evenly.
5. Bring water to a boil and blanch grapefruit peel 1 to 2 minutes to remove bitterness. Taste after 1 minute for desired flavor.
6. Drain peel under cold running water to stop cooking. Drain again on paper towels.
7. Combine grapefruit peel with 2 tablespoons of the sugar syrup.
8. Combine the remaining 2 tablespoons of the sugar and ground cloves. Remove peel from syrup with fork and coat it well on both sides with sugar-clove mixture. Transfer to cake rack and twist peel into curls. Let dry.
9. To serve, place twist of candied peel on top of each serving of ice.

Jim Fobel

To Jim Fobel, a Californian, good home cooking has an international flavor. As a child, he often visited his Japanese aunt in Hawaii; he and his parents brought back her recipes and cooked them at home. Teriyaki, a Japanese-style barbecue, was a favorite; Menu 1 features chicken teriyaki, with the traditional Japanese sauce.

At a later date, the Fobel household enjoyed Italian family feasts, prepared by Jim Fobel's sister-in-law and her mother, both of whom are Italian and excellent cooks. They often made veal scallopini—which they pounded very thin, coated in Parmesan cheese and bread crumbs, and then sautéed. Chicken cutlets take the place of veal in Menu 2.

Yet another major influence in the Fobel kitchen came from a next-door neighbor who happened to be a first-rate Mexican cook. From her, Jim Fobel learned the basics of Mexican cooking and went on to perfect a number of techniques. His specialty in Menu 3 is a quick-cooking mole sauce. This chili-based meat sauce ordinarily requires dozens of ingredients and takes hours to prepare. After much experimentation, Jim Fobel invented a recipe for mole that is ready in less than an hour.

A lacquered tray for each guest is a handsome and convenient way to serve chicken teriyaki, vegetable sushi, and rice. The flowers should be simple—a blooming branch or single bud is the right arrangement for this elegant-looking meal. Garnish the main dish with scallions, which you slice lengthwise from the center and dip in icy water so that they flare: see the ADDED TOUCH on page 59 for instructions.

57

Chicken Thighs Teriyaki
Vegetable Sushi
Rice

Ginger root is essential for this teriyaki recipe, and most supermarkets stock it in the produce department alongside the garlic and shallots. Ginger root will keep indefinitely if you slice the root and refrigerate it in a tightly capped jar filled with dry sherry.

For the vegetable sushi, you will be wrapping cooked carrots and spinach in cabbage leaves, so buy a head of cabbage with large outer leaves, which are easy to work with, and be sure the leaves are unblemished.

You will find sesame seeds and Oriental sesame oil in the supermarket but not always with the other nuts and oils. Check the international aisle or the Oriental department.

Sake is the traditional Japanese rice wine and the ingredient choice for the marinade, but a good quality dry sherry will also produce satisfactory results.

WHAT TO DRINK

A Japanese beer is good with teriyaki. Jim Fobel also recommends sake or a light white wine, such as an Italian Soave. Traditionally the Japanese serve sake warm, in a small carafe, but it is pleasant over ice as well.

SHOPPING LIST AND STAPLES

8 chicken thighs
1 large green cabbage
1½ pounds fresh spinach
2 medium-size carrots
1 large clove garlic
1 branch ginger root
½ cup plus 2 tablespoons Japanese soy sauce
2 teaspoons vegetable oil
2 teaspoons Oriental sesame oil
⅔ cup long-grain white rice
2 teaspoons cornstarch
2 tablespoons sugar
4 teaspoons toasted sesame seeds (optional)
⅔ cup sake

UTENSILS

Blender or food processor
Medium-size skillet with cover
2 medium-size saucepans with covers
Small saucepan
Broiler pan
Medium-size bowl or shallow dish
Colander
Wire strainer
Measuring cups and spoons
All-purpose knife
Paring knife
Tongs

START-TO-FINISH STEPS

1. Chop ginger root and garlic for chicken recipe.
2. Follow chicken recipe steps 1 through 4.
3. Follow rice recipe step 1.
4. Peel and shred carrots, then follow sushi recipe steps 1 through 5.
5. Follow rice recipe steps 2 and 3. As rice steams, follow chicken recipe steps 5 through 7. As chicken broils, follow sushi recipe step 6.
6. Follow chicken recipe step 8.
7. Follow sushi recipe step 7.
8. Serve chicken and sushi with rice.

RECIPES

Chicken Thighs Teriyaki

The marinade:
½ cup Japanese soy sauce
⅔ cup sake
2 slices ginger root size of quarter,
  peeled and chopped
1 large clove garlic, minced
2 tablespoons sugar

The chicken:
8 chicken thighs

The glaze:
1 cup marinade
2 teaspoons cornstarch

1. Combine all marinade ingredients in container of blender or food processor. Blend about 1 minute, or until ginger and garlic are pulverized.
2. Pour marinade through strainer set over bowl or shallow dish. Discard solids left in strainer.
3. Using your fingers (or with help of knife, if necessary), pull off and discard skin from thighs. With all-purpose knife, score meaty side of each thigh with knife strokes, about ¼ inch deep and ½ inch apart in diamond pattern.

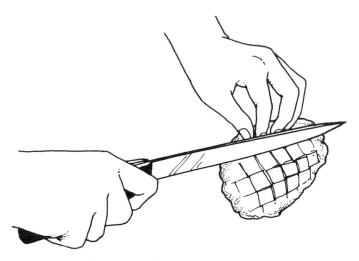

Score the thigh in diamonds with a sharp knife.

Place thighs, scored side down, in marinade. Marinate 30 minutes, turning twice.

4. After thighs have marinated 15 minutes, adjust broiler rack so it is about 5 inches from heat and preheat broiler.

5. Remove thighs from marinade and drain, letting excess marinade run back into dish. Reserve marinade. Place thighs, scored side down, in broiler pan. Broil 7 minutes.

6. Meanwhile, to make glaze, measure 1 cup marinade and place in small saucepan. Add cornstarch and stir until dissolved. Place over moderate heat and, stirring constantly, cook until mixture thickens and comes to a boil.

7. Turn thighs with tongs and broil, scored side up, 5 to 7 minutes, or until tops begin to brown and meat is cooked through. Test for doneness. Remove from broiler and arrange 2 thighs on each dinner plate.

8. Coat each thigh with about 1 tablespoon of the glaze. If desired, serve the extra teriyaki glaze in sauce boat.

Vegetable Sushi

4 green cabbage leaves (about 8 inches in diameter)
1½ pounds fresh spinach, well rinsed
2 teaspoons vegetable oil
2 medium-size carrots, peeled and coarsely shredded
   (about 1 cup)
2 teaspoons Oriental sesame oil
2 tablespoons Japanese soy sauce
4 teaspoons toasted sesame seeds (optional)
⅓ cup water

1. Bring about 1 to 2 quarts of water to a boil in medium-size saucepan over high heat.

2. Using paring knife, slice across top of each cabbage leaf to remove raised portion of vein. Submerge leaves in boiling water and cover. When boiling resumes, cook leaves about 5 minutes, or until just tender. Drain leaves on paper towels. Rinse out saucepan.

3. Trim spinach and discard stems. Place spinach in saucepan with water only clinging to leaves. Cover and place pan over moderately high heat. Cook, stirring occasionally, 2 or 3 minutes, until spinach has wilted and reduced in bulk. Drain spinach in colander and set aside.

4. Place vegetable oil in medium-size skillet over moderately high heat. Add carrots and cook, stirring constantly, 4 to 5 minutes, or until they are lightly glazed. Remove from heat and stir in sesame oil and 2 teaspoons of the soy sauce.

5. Place 4 cabbage leaves, deveined side down, on work surface. Divide spinach and arrange ¼ in flat line across lower portion of each cabbage leaf. Arrange ¼ of the carrots in line along middle of each line of spinach. Top each carrot line with 1 teaspoon of the soy sauce and 1 teaspoon of the toasted sesame seeds, if desired. Tightly roll each leaf to form cigar shape.

6. Place 4 rolls, seam side down, in skillet in which carrots cooked. Add ⅓ cup water, cover pan, and place over moderate heat. Simmer about 3 minutes, or until heated through.

7. Transfer rolls, seam side down, onto paper towels to drain before slicing. To serve, slice each roll into 6 equal pieces.

Rice

2 quarts water
⅔ cup long-grain white rice

1. Bring 2 quarts of water to a boil in medium-size saucepan.

2. When water boils, slowly add rice, a few grains at a time so water does not stop boiling. Reduce heat slightly and boil, uncovered, stirring occasionally, 12 to 15 minutes, or until rice is just tender (using fork, remove a few grains of rice from time to time to test for doneness).

3. Pour rice into strainer set over sink. Shake strainer several times to drain rice and then return rice to pan. Cover and set aside until ready to serve.

ADDED TOUCH

To make scallion brushes for garnishing the main dish, trim four scallions, cutting off the root ends and tops, leaving the scallions in three-inch lengths. Place each one on a flat surface, and with the tip of a paring knife make three or four 1-inch cuts at the root end. Turn the scallion 90 degrees and make a second set of cuts. Repeat at the leafy end, leaving about an inch of scallion uncut at its center. Drop in ice water and refrigerate until the cut parts curl into brushlike fans.

LEFTOVER SUGGESTION

The vegetable sushi uses only four large cabbage leaves, so wrap the rest in plastic and keep it for another meal. For a substantial side dish, fry two or three strips of bacon while you chop the cabbage and a medium-size yellow onion. When the bacon is crisp, break it up and add the cabbage and onions to the pan. Stir frequently, and when the vegetables begin to brown, add a teaspoon of sugar and a teaspoon of vinegar. Cook another minute, or until the cabbage and onions are golden brown.

Chicken Cutlets Parmesan
Broccoli with Lemon
Mushrooms with Basil Cream

Breading chicken breasts before you fry them seals in the juices and also results in a dinner that is as good tasting as it is nice to look at. Add pimientos to the broccoli and, at the last minute before serving, toss with butter and lemon juice.

Careful pounding and breading and quick cooking are secrets of success in the main dish here. Be sure to pound the chicken very thin. Coat each piece evenly in flour, then egg, and then in the bread crumb, cheese, and oregano mixture.

Homemade bread crumbs are better and more economical than the prepackaged kind and a good use for leftover pieces of French bread, or end pieces from loaves of packaged bread. To make bread crumbs, slice the bread into cubes and spread in a single layer on a cookie sheet. Bake at 250 degrees until the bread begins to toast. Remove the bread, let it cool, and crumble it in a blender or food processor. If you make a large batch of crumbs at a time, store them in a tightly covered jar in the refrigerator. They will stay fresh for two or three weeks.

Fresh mushrooms, available year round, need special care when you clean and trim them. Buy white or cream-colored ones, and make sure the cap curves tightly over the stem: if the gills are visible on the underside, the mushroom is past its peak. Trim the stems if necessary, and wipe the cap with a damp cloth or paper towel just before cooking. Water discolors mushrooms, so wash them quickly and with as little water as possible.

WHAT TO DRINK

The delicate flavors of this menu call for an understated and preferably Italian white wine. A dry Orvieto or a crisp Verdicchio would be a good choice. Serve them well chilled but not icy.

SHOPPING LIST AND STAPLES

4 skinless, boneless chicken breast halves
Large bunch broccoli (2 to 2½ pounds)
1 pound large fresh mushrooms
1 lemon
½ cup heavy cream
6 tablespoons butter
2 eggs
¼ pound Parmesan cheese
4-ounce jar pimientos
1 cup dry unflavored bread crumbs
⅓ cup olive oil
¼ cup flour
6 teaspoons chopped fresh oregano, or 2 teaspoons dried
3 teaspoons chopped fresh basil, or 1 teaspoon dried
Salt and pepper

¼ cup dry white wine (optional)

UTENSILS

2 large heavy skillets (1 nonaluminum)
Large heavy saucepan with cover
2 shallow bowls or pie plates
Colander
Measuring cups and spoons
Heavy cleaver or meat pounder
All-purpose knife
Slotted spoon
Juicer
Grater
Wire rack
Tongs
Waxed paper

START-TO-FINISH STEPS

1. Grate cheese and chop herbs for chicken recipe. Trim broccoli and slice pimiento for broccoli recipe.
2. Follow chicken recipe steps 1 through 4.
3. Follow broccoli recipe step 1.
4. Follow mushroom recipe step 1.
5. Follow broccoli recipe steps 2 and 3.
6. Follow mushroom recipe step 2.
7. Follow chicken recipe step 5.
8. Juice lemon and follow broccoli recipe step 4.
9. Follow mushroom recipe step 3.
10. Serve chicken with mushrooms and broccoli.

RECIPES

Chicken Cutlets Parmesan

4 skinless, boneless chicken breast halves
¼ cup flour
2 eggs
1 cup dry unflavored bread crumbs
½ cup freshly grated Parmesan cheese
6 teaspoons chopped fresh oregano, or 2 teaspoons dried
⅓ cup olive oil
Salt and freshly ground black pepper

1. Using sharp knife, remove and discard any excess fat and gristle from chicken breast. Cut away tendon from fillet (see diagram page 8, step 7). Place 1 breast half, smooth side down, on sheet of waxed paper. Top with another sheet of waxed paper. Pound cutlet until it is about ⅛ inch thick. Discard waxed paper. Repeat process with the remaining breast halves.
2. Dust pounded cutlets with flour on clean sheet of waxed paper; shake off any excess.
3. Place eggs in bowl and beat. Place bread crumbs, Parmesan cheese, and oregano in another bowl and stir together.
4. Dip each cutlet first in egg and then in crumb mixture. Set cutlets aside on wire rack until ready to cook.

5. Heat oil in skillet over moderately high heat until almost smoking. Place 2 cutlets in skillet and fry until crisp and golden brown. Turn over with tongs and fry on other side about 2 minutes. Drain on paper towels and fry remaining cutlets in same manner. Sprinkle lightly with salt and pepper.

Broccoli with Lemon

1 teaspoon salt
Large bunch broccoli (2 to 2½ pounds), trimmed and cut into flowerets
4-ounce jar pimientos, rinsed, drained, and sliced into ¼-inch strips
Salt and freshly ground black pepper
2 to 3 tablespoons lemon juice
3 tablespoons butter

1. Add salt to water and bring to a boil in covered saucepan over high heat.
2. Drop broccoli flowerets into boiling water over moderately high heat. When boiling resumes, cook 4 to 5 minutes, or until just tender.
3. Drain broccoli in colander and return to saucepan. Toss pimientos with broccoli. Add salt and pepper to taste. Cover pan and set aside.
4. Just before serving, stir lemon juice and butter into broccoli.

Mushrooms with Basil Cream

3 tablespoons butter
1 pound large mushrooms, trimmed and cut into ¼-inch slices
3 teaspoons crumbled fresh basil, or 1 teaspoon dried
¼ cup dry white wine (optional)
½ cup heavy cream
½ teaspoon salt
Freshly ground black pepper

1. Melt butter in nonaluminum skillet over moderately high heat. Add mushrooms and cook, stirring occasionally, about 5 minutes. Mushrooms will absorb butter and release some of their juices. Remove mushrooms with slotted spoon and set aside.
2. Add basil, wine—if desired—cream, salt, and pepper to skillet. Simmer over low heat about 5 minutes, or until mixture has thickened slightly.
3. Add mushrooms to cream sauce and toss to coat. Spoon onto serving plates.

ADDED TOUCH

For a quick and easy dessert, try this lemon sherbet.

Lemon Sherbet with Cassis

1 pint lemon sherbet
Crème de cassis (black currant liqueur)

Place 1 or 2 scoops of sherbet in each of 4 dessert dishes. Top each serving with 1 to 2 tablespoons crème de cassis.

Crispy Chicken Strips with Mole Sauce
Zucchini and Corn
Mexican Rice

Slivers of chicken breasts, sautéed golden, and a corn and zucchini stir fry surround a bowl of mole sauce on each dinner plate. Garnish the sauce bowls with lime slices, if desired, and pass the basket of hot tortillas and the bowl of Mexican rice.

Mole is an ancient Indian word of unknown origin and disputed meaning. According to some authorities, mole means any chili-based sauce, while others say it simply means concoction. Still others believe it is a kind of chocolate sauce—which is untrue. Although mole may indeed contain chocolate, the amount is infinitesimal, and the sauce is not sweet, but a dark and spicy mixture designed for meats, fish, rice, cheese, and vegetables. It also is added to tacos, tamales, and enchiladas.

No single definitive recipe for mole exists, and indeed there are probably as many kinds of mole sauce in Mexico as there are good cooks. The most familiar version is mole *poblano,* named for the city of Puebla, where it originated. One of its ingredients, in fact, is unsweetened chocolate, which probably gave rise to the chocolate sauce myth. In any case, it is only one of many ingredients. Recipes commonly call for as many as 20 items, and a list of 30 or more is not unusual.

The length of the ingredient list is what first attracted Jim Fobel to the sauce. "My friends and I used to play a game while we traveled," he relates. "Each of us would name one dish we would like to cook if stranded on a desert island. The goal was to think of dishes with the longest possible list of ingredients, because the winner would be entitled to a limitless supply of them during an eternal stay on the island. I always used mole *poblano* for my entry. I own an old Mexican cookbook that has a classic recipe with 35 ingredients. If all the work had to be done by hand, a recipe like that might take all day."

The Fobel version of the classic mole sauce here requires only 13 ingredients, a blender or food processor, and about 15 minutes of concentrated attention.

The seeds and spices you need should all be on the shelf in the supermarket or, if not, certainly in a health food shop. All the major spice and herb packagers sell fennel seed, anise, and cumin. Either fennel or anise is acceptable here, since both taste like licorice. Get the seed rather than the powder.

As for chili, which you use in the mole as well as in the Mexican rice, some 61 different kinds of chili plants grow in Mexico, ranging from sweet to almost unbearably hot. For this mole try to find the powdered *ancho* and *pasilla* chilis, and use a teaspoon and a half of each. Do not despair if you cannot find them. Experiment with whatever you can get, increasing the amount to suit your taste. As with any spice, store chili powder in a jar with a tight-fitting lid. Better still, keep chili powder in the refrigerator.

WHAT TO DRINK

Mexican beer, either light or dark, is ideal with this spicy meal. If you wish to serve wine, a California zinfandel, full bodied and fruity, would be perfect.

SHOPPING LIST AND STAPLES

3 whole skinless, boneless chicken breasts
2 medium-size tomatoes
1 small onion
1 small green bell pepper
4 medium-size zucchini
2 ears fresh corn
4 large cloves garlic
1 lime
3 tablespoons butter
4 to 4½ cups chicken broth
1 tablespoon unsweetened cocoa
1 package corn tortillas
1 cup long-grain white rice
9 tablespoons vegetable oil
½ cup plus 1 tablespoon flour
2 tablespoons sesame seeds
¼ cup shelled unsalted pumpkin seeds
1½ tablespoons skinless unsalted peanuts
¾ teaspoon anise seeds or fennel seeds
1½ teaspoons ground cumin seeds
3 tablespoons plus 1 teaspoon chili powder
Salt

UTENSILS

Blender or food processor
2 large heavy skillets with covers
2 medium-size heavy saucepans with covers
Measuring cups and spoons
Chef's knife
Paring knife
Tongs
Juicer

START-TO-FINISH STEPS

1. Chop onion and bell pepper and dice garlic and tomato for rice recipe.
2. Follow mole sauce recipe steps 1 through 5 (this is also

chicken recipe step 1).

3. Follow rice recipe steps 1 and 2.

4. Follow zucchini recipe steps 1 and 2.

5. Follow chicken recipe steps 2 through 7.

6. Follow zucchini recipe step 3.

7. Follow chicken recipe step 8, and serve with zucchini and rice.

RECIPES

Crispy Chicken Strips

Mole sauce (see following recipe)
2 tablespoons sesame seeds
3 whole skinless, boneless chicken breasts
4 tablespoons vegetable oil
½ cup flour
1 teaspoon salt
Corn tortillas

1. Prepare mole sauce and set aside.

2. Place sesame seeds in skillet over low heat and toast them, stirring constantly, until they are golden, about 2 minutes. Set aside. Wipe out pan with paper towel and use to cook chicken.

3. Trim away and discard any fat or gristle from chicken breasts. Cut breasts in half lengthwise and then cut each half lengthwise into ¼-inch strips.

4. Heat 2 tablespoons of the oil in skillet over moderately high heat until oil is almost smoking.

5. Place flour and salt in paper bag. Add chicken strips and shake bag to coat them with flour.

6. Without crowding pan, place about ⅓ of the strips in hot oil. Fry strips on 1 side about 3 minutes, or until crisp and deep golden brown. Working quickly, turn strips with tongs and fry for 1 minute more. Remove them and drain on paper towels.

7. Add 1 tablespoon of the remaining oil to skillet and fry half of the remaining chicken strips in same manner. Repeat with the remaining oil and chicken strips. Drain on paper towels.

8. Arrange chicken strips on platter. Sprinkle with toasted sesame seeds and serve with mole sauce and warmed tortillas.

Mole Sauce

2 to 2¼ cups chicken broth
3 tablespoons vegetable oil

1½ corn tortillas, 6 inches in diameter
¼ cup shelled unsalted pumpkin seeds
1½ tablespoons skinless unsalted peanuts
¾ teaspoon anise seeds or fennel seeds
3 large cloves garlic, crushed
1 medium-size tomato, diced
1 tablespoon flour
3 tablespoons chili powder
1½ teaspoons ground cumin seeds
1 tablespoon unsweetened cocoa
1 teaspoon salt

1. Place chicken broth in saucepan over moderately high heat until boiling; turn off heat and set aside to cool.

2. Heat oil in skillet over moderate heat until almost smoking. Using tongs, lower tortillas into oil and fry 15 seconds on each side. Let any excess oil run back into pan, and place tortillas in hot chicken broth. Turn off heat under skillet.

3. Add pumpkin seeds, peanuts, and anise or fennel seeds to hot oil in skillet. With wooden spoon, stir about 15 seconds. Pumpkin seeds should begin to pop almost immediately. Have cover on hand in case they pop too vigorously.

4. Turn heat back on to moderate. Stir in garlic and tomato and cook 1 minute. Add flour, chili powder, cumin seeds, cocoa, and salt to make thick paste. Stir constantly 1 minute and remove from heat.

5. Transfer tortillas and chicken broth and paste mixture to container of blender or food processor. Blend about 30 seconds, or until pureed. Scrape and pour mole sauce into saucepan that held chicken broth and set aside. Warm over low heat before serving. If sauce seems too thick, add several more tablespoons of chicken broth.

Zucchini and Corn

4 medium-size zucchini
2 ears fresh corn
3 tablespoons butter
1 teaspoon salt
1 tablespoon lime juice

1. Rinse zucchini and trim away ends. Cut each into ¼-inch rounds.

2. Using downward motion with knife, cut kernels of corn from cobs. It will be easier if you cut off about 3 rows at a time. You should have about 1 cup of kernels.

3. Melt butter in skillet over moderate heat. When hot but

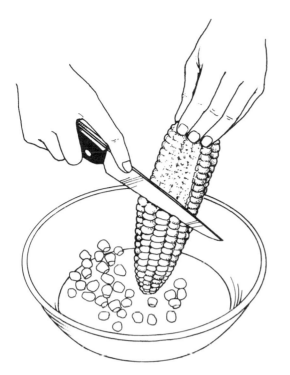

Holding cob upright, cut off kernels with a sharp knife.

not smoking, add zucchini and cook, stirring, 2 or 3 minutes until crispy. Add corn, heat, cover, and set aside. Reheat if necessary before serving, and stir in salt and lime juice.

Mexican Rice

2 tablespoons vegetable oil
1 cup long-grain white rice
1 small onion, finely chopped
1 large clove garlic, minced
1 small green bell pepper, trimmed and cut lengthwise into ¼-inch strips
1 medium-size tomato, diced
1 teaspoon chili powder
1 teaspoon salt
2 cups chicken broth

1. Heat oil in saucepan over moderate heat until almost smoking. Add rice and sauté until grains are golden brown, stirring constantly.
2. Stir in onion, garlic, and pepper strips. Sauté 1 minute. Add tomato, chili powder, and salt. Sauté another minute. Pour in chicken broth and bring mixture to a boil. Turn heat to low, cover tightly, and simmer gently 18 to 20 minutes, or until rice is just tender and liquid has been absorbed. Keep warm until served.

ADDED TOUCHES

If you have more than an hour to spend in the kitchen and want to add an appetizer or a dessert—or both—to this menu, try the following recipes: the first for an avocado in an unusual dressing, the second for a tropical confection with cream.

Sliced Avocado with Scallion Dressing

3 tablespoons fresh lime juice
½ cup olive oil
6 tablespoons minced fresh coriander or parsley
½ teaspoon salt
¼ teaspoon freshly ground black pepper
3 scallions, thinly sliced, including part of green top
1 California avocado (about 1 pound)

1. Put lime juice, oil, coriander or parsley, salt, and pepper in blender and puree. Transfer to small bowl. Stir in scallions.
2. Peel avocado and cut it in half lengthwise. Remove pit and cut each half into serving slices. Pour vinaigrette over avocado and serve.

Papaya Cream

1 papaya (about 1 pound)
¼ cup honey or ¼ cup sugar
1 tablespoon lemon or lime juice, or
    2 tablespoons dark rum
1 cup heavy cream, chilled
2 tablespoons sugar

1. Cut papaya in half lengthwise and remove and discard seeds. Scoop out pulp (there should be about 1¼ cups) and place it in container of blender or food processor. Add honey and juice, or rum, and blend to smooth puree.
2. Beat cream until soft peaks form. Add sugar and beat again until very stiff peaks form. Fold papaya puree into whipped cream, making sure they are well blended. Serve in stemmed glasses.

LEFTOVER SUGGESTION

The Mexican rice, mole, and chicken make such a delicious second-day casserole that it is worth making the meal for eight when you know you will be only four. Put leftover rice in the bottom of a casserole, add chicken pieces and mole sauce. Cover with foil and refrigerate the dish until you plan to cook it. Then preheat the oven to 350 degrees, add a cup of grated cheese (mild Cheddar or Monterey Jack), and bake for 30 to 40 minutes until the rice is hot and the cheese melts. Serve with hot tortillas.

Judith Olney

A painter and musician as well as a cook, Judith Olney believes that the colors and textures that make up a meal are as important as the flavors, and that the way you cook and serve a meal reflects your personal style as surely as the way you dress or decorate your home. In her first menu, which is Southern in every detail, the barbecued chicken, corn crisps, and black-eyed peas (all with varying golden tones) combine with the green salad to make a meal of brightly varied textures and hues: a good year-round meal, too.

Menu 2 is definitely for spring. A mixture of fresh vegetables—including asparagus, carrots, and new potatoes—surrounds steamed chicken breasts, while a *filo* dough pastry provides another variation in texture as well as in taste.

In Menu 3, the chicken cooks in the broiler, and the visual centerpiece is eggplant cut into a fan shape, filled with tomato slices, and roasted (wrapped in foil) in the oven. To ensure very ripe tomatoes, you will want to reserve this menu for summer and fall.

Fresh flowers belong on the table when you serve this meal; daisies blend particularly well with it. The corn crisps, here served in a lined bread basket, are a necessity with this meal of Southern black-eyed peas and barbecued chicken quarters. Beer goes well with this meal, and will add another bright element to the table setting.

Oven-Barbecued Chicken Quarters
Southern-Style Black-Eyed Peas
Corn Cake Crisps / Romaine Salad Vinaigrette

To some down-home Southerners, an old-style barbecue may demand a large backyard and a day's work in advance—but Judith Olney has perfected this indoor version that cooks in the oven in 45 minutes with an authentic sauce.

Black-eyed peas are a garden staple in the South, and good fresh peas come to market in late summer and fall. In other regions, fresh peas may be harder to find, but they do appear occasionally in most produce sections. If you cannot find fresh ones, the frozen kind are acceptable. Use two 8-ounce packages and follow the recipe here, but cook the peas only as long as the package specifies.

Dried black-eyed peas are another option. They are better than frozen, less expensive, and always on the supermarket shelf. Though you cannot cook them quickly, you need not spend any more actual work time on them than you would on the fresh. The package directions usually call for slow cooking and sometimes for presoaking as well. Cook them ahead and reheat them.

One way you can cook the packaged type of black-eyed peas is as follows. When you set the peas to boil, add the bacon or salt pork and the other ingredients in the Olney recipe, but not the parsley and butter. Cook the peas until almost done (taste a few on the end of a fork), remove them from the heat, and let them cool. Reheat them for 15 minutes just before the chicken comes out of the oven.

WHAT TO DRINK

Judith Olney recommends a pitcher of cold beer for this meal, since barbecue sauce and fine wines do not readily combine. But if you prefer, try a full, spicy white wine, such as a California Gewürztraminer.

SHOPPING LIST AND STAPLES

3½-pound broiler-fryer chicken, cut into quarters
1 strip bacon, or 2 pieces lean salt pork
   about 2 inches square
1 medium-size onion
1 pound shelled fresh black-eyed peas
1 large head romaine lettuce
1 clove garlic
1 bunch fresh parsley
1½ tablespoons fresh savory, or 1½ teaspoons dried
11 tablespoons butter (1 stick plus 3 tablespoons)
½ cup plus 3 tablespoons olive oil

¼ cup cider vinegar
2 tablespoons red wine vinegar
¼ cup catsup
1 cup yellow cornmeal
3 teaspoons light brown sugar
1 tablespoon paprika
Salt and pepper

UTENSILS

Large heavy skillet
2 medium-size saucepans
Small saucepan
Roasting pan
Baking sheet
Medium-size bowl
Small bowl
Salad bowl
Measuring cups and spoons
All-purpose knife

START-TO-FINISH STEPS

1. Follow chicken recipe steps 1 through 4.
2. Follow salad recipe steps 1 through 4.
3. Follow corn cake crisp recipe steps 1 through 4, except for baking.
4. Follow chicken recipe step 5. Bake corn crisp cakes (refer to step 4 of corn cake crisps recipe).
5. Follow black-eyed pea recipe steps 1 through 3.
6. Follow salad recipe step 5 and serve as first course.
7. Follow pea recipe step 3.
8. Follow chicken recipe step 6 and corn cake crisp recipe step 5. Serve both with peas.

RECIPES

Oven-Barbecued Chicken Quarters

3 tablespoons olive oil
3½-pound broiler-fryer chicken, cut into quarters
¼ cup cider vinegar
1 medium-size onion, minced
¼ cup catsup
5 tablespoons butter
1 teaspoon salt
½ teaspoon freshly ground black pepper
2 teaspoons light brown sugar

1 tablespoon paprika
Parsley sprigs for garnish (optional)

1. Preheat oven to 350 degrees.
2. Add oil to skillet and heat until almost smoking. Sauté chicken, skin side down, in oil about 10 minutes, or until lightly browned. Drain on paper towels.
3. Place remaining ingredients except parsley in medium-size saucepan and bring to a simmer, stirring. Remove from heat.
4. Transfer chicken pieces to roasting pan, placing them skin side up. Pour sauce over chicken and cover lightly with aluminum foil. Bake 20 minutes, basting frequently.
5. After 20 minutes, remove foil and turn up oven temperature to 375 degrees. Continue basting and cooking for another 25 minutes.
6. To serve, arrange chicken on platter. Skim off any fat from surface of sauce and pour sauce over chicken. Garnish with parsley sprigs, if desired.

Southern-Style Black-Eyed Peas

1 pound shelled fresh black-eyed peas
⅓ cup water
1 tablespoon salt
1 strip bacon, or 2 pieces lean salt pork
  about 2 inches square
1½ tablespoons fresh savory, or 1½ teaspoons dried
3 tablespoons butter
2 tablespoons chopped parsley

1. Place peas, water, salt, bacon or salt pork, savory, and 2 tablespoons of the butter in medium-size saucepan.
2. Bring to a boil, then simmer, uncovered, 12 to 15 minutes, or until peas are tender. By end of cooking, most of the water should have evaporated, leaving peas in buttery juice.
3. Remove bacon or salt pork. Add chopped parsley and the remaining tablespoon of butter to peas and gently swirl pan to mix ingredients. Transfer to serving dish.

Corn Cake Crisps

1 cup yellow cornmeal
½ teaspoon salt
1 teaspoon freshly ground black pepper, or to taste
1 teaspoon light brown sugar
⅔ cup water
3 tablespoons butter

1. Place cornmeal, salt, and pepper in medium-size bowl and stir.
2. Place sugar, water, and butter in small saucepan. Heat until butter has melted and then bring liquid to a rolling boil. Remove from heat.
3. Pour boiling liquid into cornmeal and stir well.
4. Lightly butter baking sheet. With large spoon, place cornmeal batter in 8 separate mounds on baking sheet. Press down on each mound with bottom of glass tumbler, which is kept floured, until each is flattened to ¼-inch-thick wafer. Bake at 375 degrees 20 minutes.
5. Serve hot with butter on the side.

Romaine Salad Vinaigrette

1 large head romaine lettuce
1 clove garlic, halved
1 teaspoon salt
½ teaspoon freshly ground black pepper
2 tablespoons red wine vinegar
½ cup olive oil

1. Rinse and thoroughly dry greens. Tear leaves into shreds. Rub salad bowl with cut garlic clove. Discard garlic.
2. Place salt, pepper, and vinegar in small bowl. Stir.
3. Stir in oil and mix well.
4. Pour dressing into salad bowl. Place greens on top of dressing and store in refrigerator until ready to serve.
5. Toss salad at table immediately before serving.

ADDED TOUCH

For a quick dessert with an original twist, mix cantaloupe with honeydew melon and serve with sherbet.

Melon with Sherbet

1 cantaloupe melon
1 honeydew melon
1 pint orange or lime sherbet
Mint sprigs (optional)

1. Cut melons in half and scoop out seeds.
2. Using melon baller, scoop 5 balls from rim of each melon half. Place orange balls in hollows of green melons; place green balls in hollows of orange melons. Refrigerate.
3. Just before serving, place scoop of sherbet in center of each melon half. Garnish with mint sprigs, if desired. and serve in glass bowls.

Herbed Cheese Pastry
Chicken Breasts with Spring Vegetables in Garlic Sauce

On curly leaf cabbage and garnished with lemon slices and parsley, steamed chicken breasts and spring vegetables look as fresh and simple as they are. A buttery garlic sauce comes on the side, along with a light pastry filled with herb cheese.

Paper thin and crunchy, *filo* dough is a Greek (the word comes from the Greek for "leaf") and Turkish specialty now available in the frozen-food section of most supermarkets. The dough, made from flour, eggs, oil, water, and salt, becomes tissue thin as the pastry chef rolls and stretches it—an exercise that takes too much time for the home cook. Buy frozen *filo* at your supermarket; the dough comes in packages of rolled-up sheets and is also called strudel dough. Keep the *filo* in your freezer until the night before you intend to use it. Then take the dough out of its box—but not out of the plastic wrap—and let it thaw in the refrigerator. As you work with the dough, remember to cover the remaining pieces with a damp cloth—or a large piece of plastic wrap—to keep it moist. Otherwise it quickly becomes brittle and impossible to handle.

You can refreeze any leftover dough. For a recipe to use it in a delicious dessert, see page 82.

Use Italian ricotta for the filling. Cottage cheese is similar but will make the tart too runny.

Savoy cabbage, or curly leaf cabbage—which makes an attractive bed for the chicken breasts and vegetables in the main dish—is available all year. Buy a head that feels heavy for its size, indicating the center is whole and healthy. The outer leaves should be fresh and free from wormholes. Use it within a day or two, since it does not stay fresh as long as regular cabbage. A curly leaf lettuce will look good, too, if it is in season.

New potatoes, carrots, scallions, mushrooms, and asparagus steam along with the chicken breasts, resulting in a dish with appealing taste and texture variety.

If you do not have a steamer large enough to hold the vegetables and chicken, turn back to page 17 for a diagram of an improvised, and very serviceable, steamer.

WHAT TO DRINK

The bright, fresh flavors of this menu need an equally fresh, slightly sweet white wine. A California Riesling or a German Riesling Kabinett would be excellent.

SHOPPING LIST AND STAPLES

4 skinless, boneless chicken breast halves
12 to 16 small new potatoes
8 small carrots with tops
8 large fresh white mushrooms
1 pound fresh asparagus
1 Savoy cabbage, or 1 head curly leaf lettuce
1 bunch scallions
1 bunch fresh parsley
2 cloves garlic
2 tablespoons chopped fresh tarragon, or
    2 teaspoons dried
3 lemons
5-ounce package cream cheese with herbs and garlic
⅓ cup ricotta cheese
13 tablespoons butter (1 stick plus 5 tablespoons)
5 eggs
6 leaves frozen *filo* pastry
1 tablespoon tarragon vinegar
Salt
Black pepper
White pepper

UTENSILS

Blender or food processor
Medium-size saucepan
Small saucepan
Shallow 8-inch round baking pan
Large vegetable steamer
    or improvised steamer
Measuring cups and spoons
Chef's knife
All-purpose knife
Metal turner
Rubber spatula
Vegetable peeler
Pastry brush
Juicer

START-TO-FINISH STEPS

The night before: remove *filo* leaves from freezer to defrost in refrigerator.

1. Follow herbed pastry recipe steps 1 through 6.
2. Follow chicken recipe steps 1 through 5.
3. Follow pastry recipe step 7. As pastry bakes, follow chicken recipe steps 6 and 7. As chicken simmers, juice lemon and follow garlic sauce recipe steps 1 through 4. Slice lemons for chicken garnish.
4. Follow pastry recipe step 8.
5. Follow chicken recipe step 8 and serve.

RECIPES

Herbed Cheese Pastry

5-ounce package cream cheese with herbs and garlic
1 egg
⅓ cup ricotta cheese
½ teaspoon salt
Freshly ground black pepper
1 tablespoon finely chopped fresh parsley
5 tablespoons butter, melted
6 leaves frozen *filo* pastry, defrosted

1. Preheat oven to 375 degrees.
2. Combine herbed cream cheese, egg, ricotta, salt, pepper, and parsley in blender or food processor and blend until smooth. Scrape sides of bowl if necessary.
3. Using pastry brush, brush bottom and sides of baking pan with melted butter. Keeping remaining sheets of *filo* covered with damp cloth as you work, line pan with sheet of *filo* pastry. Let pastry hang over sides but fit and press it neatly inside pan. Brush sheet with butter. Place 4 more sheets in pan, buttering each sheet as added. There should be no holes or open spaces where pan shows through.
4. Spread cheese filling over *filo*.
5. Place ½ sheet of *filo* over cheese. Brush *filo* lightly with butter. Loosely fold up overhanging *filo* to enclose cheese—rough and rustic surface will look best.
6. Brush other ½ sheet of *filo* with butter and roll it up. Twist it into rough rosette and place on top in center for decoration. Brush top of pastry with butter.
7. Bake 20 minutes, or until pastry is golden brown.
8. To serve, run knife around edge of pan. Carefully lift pastry out with metal turner and place on serving dish. Cut into 4 pieces and serve hot as first course.

Chicken Breasts with Spring Vegetables

12 to 16 small new potatoes
8 small carrots with tops
1 bunch scallions
8 large fresh white mushrooms
2 lemons
1 pound fresh asparagus
4 skinless, boneless chicken breast halves
Salt and freshly ground black pepper
2 tablespoons chopped fresh tarragon, or
    2 teaspoons dried
1 Savoy cabbage, or 1 head curly leaf lettuce
1 tablespoon finely chopped fresh parsley (optional)
Garlic sauce (see following recipe)

1. Bring salted water to a boil in medium-size saucepan.
2. Peel potatoes. Cut off all but 2 inches from green carrot tops. Scrape carrots with vegetable peeler and trim so that they are uniformly 3 to 4 inches long. Trim scallions, leaving 2 inches of green.
3. Place potatoes in boiling water and cook 5 minutes. Add

carrots and scallions and cook another 5 minutes.
4. Trim ends of mushroom stems. Gently rub caps of whole mushrooms with cut half of lemon.
5. Break asparagus stalks at their tender points and rinse well. Discard tough stalks.
6. Fill large vegetable steamer with water to just below steamer rack. Lightly grease rack. Steamer must be large enough to hold chicken and vegetables in 1 layer without crowding them; if not large enough, prepare in 2 batches.
7. Place chicken, asparagus, and mushrooms in center of steamer rack, with carrots, scallions, and potatoes around them. Sprinkle with salt, pepper, and tarragon. Cover and steam 15 minutes. Check to see if chicken and vegetables are done; if not, steam several minutes more.
8. Arrange cabbage or lettuce leaves on serving platter. Place chicken breasts in center of leaves and group vegetables around them. Sprinkle potatoes and mushrooms lightly with chopped parsley and garnish with lemon slices, as desired. Serve garlic sauce separately.

Garlic Sauce

8 tablespoons butter (1 stick)
4 eggs yolks, at room temperature
1 tablespoon tarragon vinegar
4 teaspoons lemon juice
2 cloves garlic
½ teaspoon salt
1 tablespoon finely chopped fresh parsley
White pepper

1. Melt butter in small saucepan.
2. Place egg yolks, tarragon vinegar, lemon juice, garlic, and salt in blender or food processor and mix to incorporate all ingredients.
3. With motor on, slowly pour in melted butter.
4. When sauce has thickened, stir in minced parsley. Add salt and white pepper to taste.

ADDED TOUCHES

Fresh strawberries should be in season about the same time as the main-course asparagus. So, if you want a dessert, try this quick recipe.

Strawberry-Orange Parfait

1 pint orange sherbet
½ pint fresh strawberries
Sugar

1. Put sherbet in refrigerator to soften.
2. Wash and hull berries, setting aside 4 perfect berries for garnish.
3. Place berries in container of blender or food processor and blend to chunky stage. Add sugar to taste.
4. Place 1 tablespoon berries in bottom of each parfait glass. Add small scoop of softened sherbet and flatten it in glass. Add 2 tablespoons strawberries and another scoop of sherbet. Top each parfait with whole strawberry.

Broiled Chicken with Sage Butter
Eggplant Fans with Tomatoes
Cucumber Salad with Sour Cream

Garden fresh vegetables make a centerpiece here. Garnish the platter with the same vegetables that you used in the meal.

Broiled chicken quarters with side dishes of fresh vegetables make a delicious warm-weather meal. Sage, an aromatic, easy-to-grow herb, complements poultry. You should use it sparingly because it can overpower the chicken's subtle flavor.

Eggplants taste best when they weigh one pound or less. Bigger ones tend to have more seeds and less flavor. Pick firm eggplants with a satiny shine and store them in a plastic bag in the refrigerator.

For a more leisurely company meal, you may decide to cook the chicken on an outdoor grill. If so, coordinate your indoor salad and eggplant preparations. To serve, arrange chicken and eggplant on dinner plates and pass the sage butter and the cucumber salad.

WHAT TO DRINK

The cook recommends a dry rosé served over ice. Because of the range of flavors here, a full-bodied California Chardonnay or a light young Beaujolais could also be served.

SHOPPING LIST AND STAPLES

3½- to 4-pound broiler-fryer chicken
2 small eggplants (4 to 5 inches long)

73

2 small firm tomatoes
2 large cucumbers
1 head romaine lettuce
1 clove garlic
1 bunch watercress, or fresh basil (optional)
24 chopped fresh sage leaves, or 2½ teaspoons dried
1 lemon
⅔ cup sour cream
4 tablespoons butter
¼ cup olive oil
1 tablespoon chopped fresh oregano, or 1 teaspoon dried
Salt and pepper
3 tablespoons dry white wine

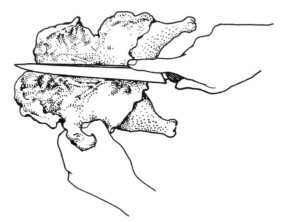

With chef's knife, remove backbone of chicken.

UTENSILS

Baking pan
Small heavy skillet
Large platter
3 small bowls
1 medium-size bowl
Small fine strainer
Measuring cups and spoons
Large chef's knife or poultry shears
All-purpose knife
Pastry brush
Vegetable peeler
Tongs

START-TO-FINISH STEPS

1. Cut garlic, chop sage, and juice lemon for chicken recipe. Follow chicken recipe steps 1 through 5.
2. Chop oregano and follow eggplant recipe steps 1 through 5, except for baking.
3. Juice lemon; follow cucumber recipe steps 1 through 4.
4. Follow chicken recipe steps 6 and 7. Also bake eggplant (refer to step 5 of eggplant recipe).
5. Follow sage butter recipe steps 1 and 2.
6. Follow cucumber recipe step 5.
7. Follow chicken recipe step 8.
8. Follow eggplant recipe step 6 and serve with chicken and cucumber salad.

RECIPES

Broiled Chicken

3½- to 4-pound broiler-fryer chicken

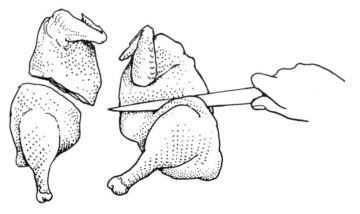

Tuck wing tips in and slice chicken into quarters.

4 chopped fresh sage leaves, or ½ teaspoon dried
1 clove garlic, cut in half
¼ cup olive oil
3 tablespoons dry white wine
Juice of ½ lemon
1 teaspoon salt
Freshly ground black pepper
Sage butter (see following recipe)

1. Preheat broiler.
2. Using large chef's knife or poultry shears, remove backbone from chicken by cutting down one side of bone and then other. Tuck and fold wing tips back under long wing bone at top of bird. Cut chicken into quarters. Trim and discard any excess fat from bird.
3. Loosen skin over breast and insert sage leaves between skin and meat.
4. Place chicken on platter. Rub cut clove of garlic over skin of chicken to flavor it.
5. Combine oil, wine, lemon juice, salt, and pepper in small bowl. Brush heavily over bird and let it sit in marinade until time to broil. Reserve marinade that collects on platter.

6. Place chicken quarters, skin side down, on foil-lined baking pan. Broil chicken at least 5 to 6 inches from heat source, until brown, about 15 to 20 minutes for each side.
7. Baste liberally with reserved marinade.
8. Remove to serving platter. Pour sage butter over chicken.

Sage Butter

4 tablespoon butter
20 chopped fresh sage leaves, or 2 teaspoons dried

1. Melt butter in skillet over medium heat.
2. Add sage leaves, then allow butter to cook until brown color. If using dried sage, strain butter through small fine strainer and discard sage. Reserve butter.

Eggplant Fans with Tomatoes

⅓ cup olive oil
2 small eggplants (4 to 5 inches long)
2 small firm tomatoes
Salt
Freshly ground black pepper
1 tablespoon chopped fresh oregano, or 1 teaspoon dried
Watercress, or fresh basil sprigs, for garnish (optional)

1. Cut 2 sheets of aluminum foil about 15 inches long. Oil well on 1 side with 1 tablespoon of the oil.
2. Rinse and dry eggplants. Trim off stems and cut in half lengthwise. Place halves cut side down. Leaving an inch of stem end whole and uncut, slice each half lengthwise into 6 to 8 thin fanned strips. Place the 2 halves, cut side down, on each piece of oiled foil.
3. Slice tomatoes very thin and place slices between fans of eggplant.
4. Season with salt, pepper, and oregano. Sprinkle the remaining olive oil generously over eggplants.
5. Fold up foil and twist edges together. Place on lowest rack of oven and cook 30 minutes, or until cooked through.
6. To serve, place 1 eggplant half on each plate and garnish stem end with sprigs of watercress or basil, as desired.

Cucumber Salad with Sour Cream

2 large cucumbers
2 teaspoons salt
Juice of ½ lemon
⅔ cup sour cream
Freshly ground black pepper
Large outer leaves of romaine lettuce

1. Peel cucumbers and slice in half lengthwise. Scoop out central seedy portions with spoon and discard, then slice cucumbers thinly.
2. Place cucumber slices in small bowl and sprinkle with salt in order to draw out excess liquid. Mix well. Place bowl in freezer 10 minutes.
3. Squeeze cucumber slices by handfuls until they are as dry as possible.
4. Stir lemon juice into sour cream in small bowl. Add freshly ground pepper to taste. Stir in cucumber and taste for seasoning. Add salt if necessary. Chill until served.
5. Line serving dish with romaine leaves and spoon cucumber into middle.

ADDED TOUCHES

You can vary the cucumber salad in several interesting ways. Add finely chopped fresh dill to the sour cream for a completely different taste. Or use yogurt instead of sour cream and season with dill or with freshly grated ginger.

Oregano is not the only herb that goes well with the eggplant. Try adding tarragon or a mixture of ground cumin and cinnamon to the eggplant before and after you broil or grill it.

For dessert, combine peaches, banana, coconut, and an orange liqueur, as follows.

Peach Ambrosia

1 tablespoon lemon juice
3 tablespoons light brown sugar
3 to 4 ripe freestone peaches
2 ripe bananas
Grand Marnier (optional)
½ cup shredded coconut

1. Combine lemon juice and sugar in serving bowl and stir to mix well.
2. Peel peaches and slice into serving bowl.
3. Peel and slice bananas into bowl and mix fruits gently. Sprinkle with Grand Marnier, if desired, and chill.
4. Before serving, toast coconut under broiler or in dry skillet until light brown. Sprinkle over fruit.

Paula Wolfert

A cookbook author and a longtime resident of both France and Morocco, Paula Wolfert specializes in Mediterranean cooking. Of the three chicken dishes in the menus that follow, two are regional French and one distinctively modern French. In Menu 1, the chicken with green grapes and whole cloves of garlic is an adaptation of an old springtime specialty from southwestern France. The underripe grapes retain their tartness in cooking, but the garlic releases its flavor and turns sweet.

In Menu 2, chicken breasts combine smoothly with artichoke hearts and a cream sauce that takes its particular piquancy from sherry wine vinegar. Cream sauces thickened with egg yolks will curdle if you boil them, so use a gentle flame (or low setting on an electric range) as you add the cream to the sauté pan and follow the tip in the recipe: beat a tablespoon of cold water into the egg yolk before adding it to the hot sauce.

In Menu 3, the modern French one, Paula Wolfert flattens boned chicken breasts, steams them, and coats them with a rich creamy sauce strongly flavored with the juice from clementines. These small, intensely sweet relatives of tangerines (which you may substitute in this recipe if clementines are not available) are native to southern Spain, Morocco, and Algeria. They ripen only in the winter months, and even the largest market may not stock them regularly. Ask the produce manager to stock clementines when they are available.

Dished up together on a large platter, chicken with green grapes, and potatoes cooked in their skins, accompanied by a green salad, provide a celebratory dinner for spring, when the key ingredients—tart grapes and new potatoes—are fresh in the marketplace.

Sautéed Chicken with Tart Green Grapes
New Potatoes with Herbs
Green Salad Vinaigrette

One of the great regional cooking traditions of France grew up in the southwest around the Dordogne River. Chicken with tart or sour green grapes is an old favorite there; cooks call the piquant liquid pressed from grapes *ver jus* ("green juice") and use it in other dishes besides chicken.

Since most grapes in American markets have been picked for eating, not cooking, you may have to search for really tart grapes. Be sure to taste them before buying. If the grapes you find are not tart enough, add a few drops of lemon juice to the dish just before you serve it; the sauce must not taste sweet if it is to be authentic.

Cooking with unpeeled garlic cloves is an eminently easy and useful technique that produces an agreeably different result from mincing or chopping the garlic. Cooked in its skin, the garlic tends to lose its characteristic strong flavor, and instead contributes a savory aroma and taste, finally turning mild—as unlike raw garlic as a cooked onion is unlike a raw one. You should encourage your guests to mash the cloves with their forks, releasing the creamy juices.

Properly cooked breast meat has a silky sheen and will be firm to the touch. Train yourself to test by touch: you will soon become infallible and will never need to pierce a thigh or breast. (You may want to refer to the testing-for-doneness instructions on page 9.)

When you buy new potatoes, avoid those with green spots—they taste sour. To keep green spots from forming after you have brought the potatoes home, store them away from heat, light, and dampness. Use new potatoes as soon as possible—they will not keep as long as baking potatoes. And, for easy cooking, pick out potatoes of a uniform size. Otherwise, they will not cook evenly.

WHAT TO DRINK

This spring dish with green grapes needs a very dry, crisp wine, such as a California Sauvignon Blanc. A Sancerre would also go well with this meal.

SHOPPING LIST AND STAPLES

3-pound chicken, quartered
1 to 1½ pounds small new potatoes
1 head Boston lettuce
8 cloves garlic
1 teaspoon chopped fresh chives, or ½ teaspoon

freeze-dried
1 bunch fresh parsley
¾ pound seedless tart green grapes
1 lemon
6 tablespoons butter
3 cups chicken broth
2¼ teaspoons sherry wine vinegar or red wine vinegar
2 tablespoons walnut oil
4 tablespoons olive oil
Salt and pepper
3 tablespoons dry white wine

UTENSILS

Blender or food processor
Large deep nonaluminum skillet with cover
Large heavy skillet with cover
Small saucepan
Small bowl
Strainer
Measuring cups and spoons
Chef's knife
Tongs
Vegetable brush
Whisk
Juicer

START-TO-FINISH STEPS

1. Juice lemon and follow salad recipe steps 1 and 2. Set aside.
2. Follow chicken recipe steps 1 through 6. As chicken cooks, follow potato recipe step 1. Chop parsley and chives.
3. Follow chicken recipe steps 7 and 8. As chicken continues cooking, follow potato recipe step 2.
4. Follow chicken recipe steps 9 and 10.
5. Follow salad recipe step 3 and potato recipe step 3. Serve both with chicken.

RECIPES

Sautéed Chicken with Tart Green Grapes

2 cups chicken broth
3-pound chicken, quartered
Salt and freshly ground black pepper
1½ cups seedless tart green grapes (about ¾ pound)

3 tablespoons butter
8 plump cloves garlic, unpeeled
3 tablespoons dry white wine
2 teaspoons chopped fresh parsley

1. In saucepan, simmer chicken broth until it is reduced to ⅔ cup. Set aside.
2. While broth is simmering, cut away and discard any excess fat from chicken quarters. Rub chicken with salt and pepper and set aside.
3. Puree 1 cup of the grapes in blender or food processor for 20 seconds. Rub puree through strainer, using back of wooden spoon to press some of pulp through. You should have about ¼ cup green-grape juice. Discard pureed pulp.
4. In large deep nonaluminum skillet, heat 2 tablespoons of the butter over high heat. Add chicken pieces, skin side down, and unpeeled garlic cloves. Brown chicken pieces 1 minute on each side. Shake pan often to keep chicken pieces and garlic from sticking.
5. Lower heat, cover pan tightly, and cook 10 minutes.
6. Uncover pan, tilt it, and degrease juices. Turn chicken with tongs and add white wine to pan. Cover and cook over low heat 10 minutes longer.
7. Uncover pan and add 3 tablespoons of the grape juice. Cover again quickly so chicken pieces absorb all aroma and flavor. Cook chicken about 7 minutes more.
8. Test breast quarters for doneness and remove them from skillet. Cover them lightly to keep warm and moist. Add ½ cup of the reduced chicken stock to skillet. Continue to cook leg quarters and garlic, uncovered, 5 minutes more, or until done. There should be about ¼ cup of juice in skillet. Return breast pieces to pan. Turn chicken and garlic cloves in syrupy pan juices in order to glaze them. Remove chicken from skillet. Cover and keep warm in oven while you make sauce.
9. Raise heat and add the remaining chicken stock, the remaining 1 tablespoon of butter, the remaining juice, and the remaining ½ cup grapes. Swirl over heat to combine. Remove from heat and season with salt and pepper.
10. Arrange chicken, garlic, and grapes on serving platter. Spoon sauce over them. Sprinkle with parsley.

New Potatoes with Herbs

1 to 1½ pounds small new potatoes, unpeeled
1 cup chicken broth
3 tablespoons butter
Salt
1 teaspoon chopped fresh parsley
1 teaspoon chopped fresh chives, or ½ teaspoon
   freeze-dried

1. Scrub potatoes with brush. Arrange them in large heavy skillet in 1 layer. They must fit snugly. Pour in broth and bring to a boil. Cover tightly and cook about 4 minutes, shaking skillet over high heat until almost all liquid has evaporated.
2. Lower heat, add butter, and cook gently 10 minutes, uncovered, shaking skillet often. Test for doneness with fork. Partly cover and set aside; keep warm.

3. Sprinkle with salt, chopped parsley, and chives just before serving.

Green Salad Vinaigrette

1 head Boston lettuce
2¼ teaspoons sherry wine vinegar or red wine vinegar
2¼ teaspoons lemon juice
¼ teaspoon salt
Freshly ground black pepper
6 tablespoons oil, preferably 2 tablespoons walnut oil and
   4 tablespoons olive oil

1. Wash and dry salad greens. Refrigerate.
2. Combine vinegar and lemon juice in bowl. Add salt and pepper. Whisk in oil.
3. Just before serving, toss lettuce with vinaigrette.

ADDED TOUCHES

For a simple first course, trim off ends and string a pound of snow peas, sauté them very briefly in butter, drain, and cool. Roast, peel, and seed one ripe, sweet red pepper and cut it into julienne strips. Slice four scallions thinly and arrange the vegetables on four serving plates. Make a vinaigrette according to the salad recipe on this page and add 1 tablespoon of Dijon-style mustard. Spoon over the vegetables and serve.

A sabayon is a rich, creamy sauce, based on egg yolks, that French cooks typically use for fruit desserts. This version is particularly good with strawberries and will be even better if the strawberries are fresh picked in spring. If you have to buy strawberries in a market, choose berries in a container with no red stains, which are a sign the berries may be old. And take a quick look at the berries at the bottom, to be sure they are not squashy and overripe. To wash strawberries quickly, immerse them in cold water for half a minute, then rinse under running water and drain thoroughly.

Strawberries with Sabayon

1 pint fresh strawberries
4 eggs yolks
¼ cup superfine sugar
Juice of ½ orange
1½ tablespoons Triple Sec or Grand Marnier
2 to 3 tablespoons heavy cream

1. Wipe strawberries with damp paper towels. Hull and set side by side in heat-proof serving dish, pointed side up.
2. Beat yolks in double boiler over simmering water. Add sugar and whisk until smooth, continuing until mixture starts to thicken. Never let mixture reach a boil.
3. Add orange juice and whisk mixture until it thickens again. Repeat with Triple Sec and cream.
4. Cool sauce pot on bed of ice, stirring sauce to keep it from getting lumpy.
5. Coat berries with sauce and run serving dish under broiler just to glaze sauce. Serve at once.

Chicken Breasts and Artichokes with Fettuccine
Green Salad Vinaigrette

Chicken breasts, artichoke hearts, fettuccine, and cream sauce should arrive at the table all together on one platter. You will want separate plates for the salad, however, which is a mixture of three greens in a vinaigrette dressing.

Because it is time consuming to prepare fresh artichokes, Paula Wolfert suggests using frozen artichoke hearts. They will certainly save time, and their flavor is quite adequate if you buy a high-quality brand. But if you have an extra 15 minutes, substitute fresh artichoke hearts; they taste better than frozen. For a quick method of turning an artichoke into an artichoke heart, see the ADDED TOUCH on page 82.

The guiding principle of the salad here is to combine one or more crisp green with a pale leafy lettuce. The mix that Paula Wolfert specifies is chicory, escarole, and *radicchio*, but do choose any combination of available greens that appeals to you. Chicory, which the greengrocer may also call curly endive, has very curly outer leaves of dark green and a slightly bitter taste. Escarole has a flat-edged leaf with all the crispness of chicory—and its own slightly sharp taste. *Radicchio*, a red-leaved wild chicory, faintly bitter and pleasantly aromatic, is a garden favorite that does not travel well. Use it the same day you buy it.

The special oil and vinegar in this recipe may prove hard to find, and they are certainly expensive. But you should treat yourself and your guests to them if you can: walnut oil, pressed from green walnuts, has a taste that cannot be duplicated; buy in small quantities, and once you have opened the bottle or tin, refrigerate it. But if these ingredients are too hard to come by, you may safely substitute a good olive oil and a red wine vinegar.

WHAT TO DRINK

Like asparagus, artichokes do not combine well with wine, but the creamy sauce on the artichokes in this menu makes them compatible with a full-bodied wine, for example an Italian or Californian Chardonnay.

SHOPPING LIST AND STAPLES

4 skinless, boneless chicken breast halves
1 small head chicory
1 small head escarole
1 small head *radicchio*
1 bunch fresh parsley
1 lemon
6 tablespoons butter
½ cup heavy cream
1 egg
9-ounce package frozen artichoke hearts
1 pound fresh or packaged fettuccine or *tagliatelle*
1 cup chicken broth
2 tablespoons walnut oil
4 tablespoons olive oil
Sherry wine vinegar or red wine vinegar
Salt and pepper

UTENSILS

Large saucepan with cover
Large nonaluminum skillet with cover
2 small bowls
Measuring cups and spoons
Colander
All-purpose knife
Long-pronged fork
Whisk
Juicer

START-TO-FINISH STEPS

1. If fixing fresh artichokes, follow explanation on page 82; otherwise, defrost frozen artichokes. Chop parsley for chicken recipe and juice lemon for salad recipe.
2. Follow salad recipe steps 1 and 2.
3. Follow chicken recipe steps 1 through 8.
4. Follow salad recipe step 3, and serve with chicken.

RECIPES

Chicken Breasts and Artichokes with Fettuccine

4 skinless, boneless chicken breast halves
Salt and freshly ground black pepper
6 tablespoons butter
2 to 3 tablespoons sherry wine vinegar or red wine vinegar
9-ounce package frozen artichoke hearts, defrosted
1 cup chicken broth
½ cup heavy cream
1 pound fresh or packaged fettuccine or *tagliatelle*
1 egg yolk
1 tablespoon water
1 tablespoon chopped fresh parsley

1. In covered saucepan, bring salted water to a boil for pasta.
2. Thoroughly dry chicken breasts. Rub with salt and pepper. Heat 1 tablespoon of the butter in nonaluminum skillet over low heat. Add chicken breasts and sprinkle them with 1 tablespoon of the vinegar. Cover and cook over low heat 3 minutes on each side or until cooked through. Remove breasts from pan and transfer to plate; keep warm by covering with foil.
3. Add another tablespoon of the butter to skillet. Add artichoke hearts and sauté over medium-high heat 2 minutes, or until tender. Remove artichokes from skillet and set aside.
4. Deglaze pan by stirring 1 tablespoon of the vinegar into skillet. Add chicken broth and simmer, stirring, until broth is reduced by ½.
5. Add cream, stirring, and reduce liquid again by ⅓.
6. Add fettuccine to boiling water and stir several times with long-pronged fork. Cook 5 to 8 minutes. (If using fresh fettucine, cook according to maker's instructions.) Drain in colander and return to saucepan. Toss with the remaining 4 tablespoons butter. Season to taste.
7. Beat egg yolk in small bowl with 1 tablespoon cold water for 45 seconds, or until foamy. Then whisk it into hot sauce

in skillet. Immediately remove skillet from heat, whisking constantly. Sauce must not boil after eggs are added. Adjust seasoning with salt and pepper and, if desired, a drop more vinegar to taste. Stir in parsley.

8. Arrange chicken halves and artichoke hearts on bed of fettuccine. Spoon sauce over them.

Green Salad Vinaigrette

1 small head chicory
1 small head escarole
1 small head *radicchio*
2¼ teaspoons sherry wine vinegar or red wine vinegar
2¼ teaspoons lemon juice
¼ teaspoon salt
Freshly ground black pepper
6 tablespoons oil, preferably 2 tablespoons walnut oil and
    4 tablespoons olive oil

1. Wash and dry salad greens. Refrigerate.

2. Combine vinegar and lemon juice in small bowl. Add salt and pepper. Whisk in oil.

3. Just before serving, toss salad greens with vinaigrette.

ADDED TOUCHES

For an elegant dessert, try this croustade: butter, rum, and crushed walnuts in *filo*, or strudel, dough.

Walnut and Rum Croustade

1¼ cups freshly shelled walnut halves
½ cup dry, unflavored bread crumbs
½ teaspoon grated lemon rind
½ cup plus 1 tablespoon superfine sugar
8 tablespoons butter (1 stick), melted
¼ cup dark rum
8 *filo* pastry leaves

1. Grind walnuts in food processor. Add bread crumbs, lemon rind, and ½ cup of the sugar and process until well blended. Mix in 2 tablespoons of the melted butter and rum.

2. Preheat oven to 375 degrees.

3. Brush 8-inch round cake or pie tin with a bit of the remaining melted butter. Cover bottom of pan with 1 sheet of *filo* dough. Fit dough in pan and brush lightly with butter. Layer 5 more sheets of the dough on top, brushing each lightly with butter and scattering each with ⅕ of walnut mixture.

4. Cover with the 2 remaining sheets of dough, brushing each with butter. Tuck them in around edges. Brush top with butter and bake 35 to 45 minutes, or until golden in color and crisp.

5. Sprinkle the remaining 1 tablespoon of sugar on top and let stand on cake rack 15 minutes. Cut into wedges and serve warm.

Fresh Artichokes

Three or four large fresh artichokes—if you are going to use fresh rather than frozen—will be sufficient for this recipe. Make this the first of your START-TO-FINISH STEPS.

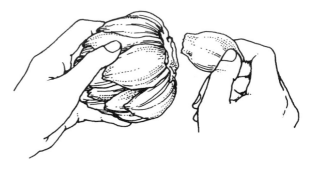

Cut off stem. Pull off the hard outer leaves from the bottom. Bring enough water to cover the artichokes to a boil in a large pot and, meanwhile, soak the artichokes in cold water. Cook the artichokes at a simmer for 15 minutes, or until you can remove a leaf easily. Drain and set aside until cool enough to handle.

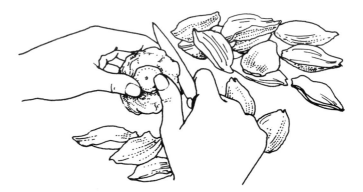

Pull away all remaining leaves above the bottom, and trim any remaining stem and leafy bit from the underside. Reserve leaves if desired.

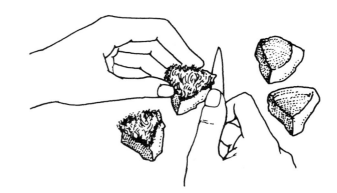

Cut the bottom into quarters. Carefully run the tip of a knife under the fuzzy choke or pull off the choke with your hands and discard. If desired, the tender edible portion of the leaves can be eaten if reserved leaves are boiled an additional 15–20 minutes. Set aside the quartered artichoke hearts until time to sauté them (step 3 of the chicken recipe).

Steamed Chicken Sausages with Broccoli in Clementine Sauce
Rice

The sauce here takes its color from clementines—or from tangerines. The sections of either fruit make an attractive garnish.

The chicken sausages in this recipe are not sausages at all but boneless chicken breasts pounded thin and rolled into a sausage shape, with half a teaspoon of butter inside each roll. Like almost any form of steamed chicken, they present the opportunity to make a colorful, highly flavored sauce—in this case, a clementine sauce with a chicken broth and cream base.

Clementines come from Spain and Morocco and are a cross between a tangerine and a small variety of orange. American markets carry them only from November through February and not regularly even then. Like truffles, they are a rarity, usually expensive but with an unforgettable aroma and sweetness. If you can find them, be choosy when you select them. Look for those with a deep orange coloring and with thin, smooth skins. And avoid any fruit with soft spots or mold. Pick out clementines that seem heavy for their size, since those will probably be the juiciest.

If you cannot lay hands upon clementines, this recipe will be delicious—if not quite so unusual—with tangerines. And if fresh tangerines are not in season, or if you are really in a hurry, try frozen tangerine concentrate. Do not reconstitute it with water but, instead, use about a third of the can of concentrate and add no liquid except a teaspoon of lemon juice.

Although clementines and tangerines are both very sweet, they blend like magic with the cream, broth, butter, salt, and pepper, and after the sauce has cooked, you will discover that most of the sweetness has disappeared. The result is a complex, even mysterious, flavor.

Plain as they are, broccoli and rice make the best side dishes for this unusual main dish. Broccoli is available all year; buy green heads with firm stems and compact bud clusters. Store broccoli in plastic in the refrigerator. And since broccoli is an excellent source of two highly perishable vitamins (A and C), use it within three days.

WHAT TO DRINK

The sweet-tart flavors of the clementine sauce need a white wine with the slightest hint of sweetness to accompany them: a California Riesling or a German Riesling Kabinett or a California Chenin Blanc.

SHOPPING LIST AND STAPLES

8 skinless, boneless chicken breast halves
1 bunch broccoli
5 medium-size clementines or tangerines
1 lemon (optional)
10 tablespoons butter (1¼ sticks)
½ cup heavy cream
1 cup chicken broth
1 cup long-grain white rice
Salt and pepper

UTENSILS

Medium-size saucepan with cover
Small nonaluminum saucepan
Small saucepan
Large steamer or large saucepan with steaming rack
Measuring cups and spoons
Meat pounder or heavy cleaver
Chef's knife
Long-pronged fork
Waxed paper
Heat-proof plastic wrap
Tongs
Juicer

START-TO-FINISH STEPS

1. Cut broccoli into flowerets for chicken recipe.
2. Follow clementine sauce recipe steps 1 and 2.
3. Follow rice recipe steps 1 and 2. As rice simmers, follow chicken recipe steps 1 and 2. As chicken steams, follow clementine sauce recipe step 3.
4. Follow rice recipe step 3.
5. Follow chicken recipe steps 3 and 4.
6. Follow clementine sauce recipe step 4.
7. Follow chicken recipe step 5 and serve with rice.

RECIPES

Steamed Chicken Sausages with Broccoli

8 skinless, boneless chicken breast halves
Salt and freshly ground black pepper
4 teaspoons butter, softened
1 bunch broccoli, separated into flowerets, stems removed
2 tablespoons butter, melted
Clementine sauce (see following recipe)

1. Gently pound chicken breasts between sheets of waxed paper until they are uniform in size and thin enough to roll. Season each breast with salt and pepper, and spread each breast with ½ teaspoon of softened butter. Roll each breast, starting at narrow end, into shape of sausage, enclosing butter. Squeeze gently so that each rolled sausage adheres and stays rolled. Wrap each in heat-proof plastic wrap and twirl ends to seal.
2. Add small amount of water to steamer or large saucepan with rack. Do not let water touch rack. Bring water to a boil. Using tongs, carefully arrange chicken and broccoli on rack in 1 layer. Cover and steam 9 to 12 minutes, depending on size of breasts.
3. Remove chicken from plastic wrap and cut into 2 or 3 equal slices.
4. Remove broccoli to serving dish. Season and sprinkle with melted butter.
5. Arrange chicken slices on warmed serving plates. Coat with clementine sauce.

Clementine Sauce

5 medium-size clementines or tangerines (enough to make 1 cup strained juice), or ⅓ cup frozen tangerine concentrate
1 cup chicken broth

½ cup heavy cream
2 to 3 tablespoons butter
Salt and freshly ground black pepper
Lemon juice (optional)

1. Squeeze clementines and strain juice. In nonaluminum saucepan, reduce juice to ⅓ cup over low heat.
2. Add chicken broth to clementine juice (or frozen tangerine concentrate) and bring to a boil. Cook until reduced by ½.
3. Add cream and reduce again until sauce is just thick enough to coat spoon. Set aside.
4. Just before serving, reheat, and swirl butter into sauce. Adjust seasonings with salt and pepper and, if too sweet, a touch of lemon juice.

Rice

2 cups salted water
1 cup long-grain white rice
4 tablespoons butter
Salt and freshly ground black pepper

1. In medium-size saucepan, bring 2 cups salted water to a boil.
2. Add rice and bring water back to a boil. Stir with long-pronged fork to separate grains. Reduce heat to low, cover tightly, and simmer 20 minutes, or until all water is absorbed.
3. Add butter to cooked rice and toss. Season with salt and pepper. Keep warm until served.

ADDED TOUCHES

If you want a first course, serve a fresh fennel appetizer. Two small fennel bulbs will make four servings (see fennel drawing on page 96). Remove the tops and cut away the hard outer stalks. Trim each base and thinly slice. Cover with ice water and refrigerate until serving time. Then make a mustard cream dressing:

1 lemon, juiced (about 3 tablespoons)
3 tablespoons heavy cream
1 tablespoon Dijon mustard
Salt and pepper to taste

Combine all ingredients in small bowl, using wire whisk. Drain fennel, and spoon dressing over each serving. Garnish with chopped parsley and walnut halves, if desired.

Since the main course is rather light, a substantial dessert might be welcome with this meal. This combination of pineapple, brioche, and ice cream is easy to make and a good complement to a meal that contains a distinctive fruit flavor also. Use only fresh pineapple, and look for the Hawaiian kind, which is better than other imports. Once picked, a pineapple will not continue to ripen, so be sure to buy a fruit that is at its peak. Pick it up and smell it—it should be fragrant and sweet; but if the bottom has a slightly fermented smell, then it is overripe.

Brioche, called for in this recipe, is a French cakelike bread of yeast dough that is baked in a high-walled, fluted pan. Good bakeries always sell them. This is a good way to use up day-old brioches, which will toast nicely and stay crisp in the rum-flavored sauce. If you use pound cake, toast it as you do the brioche.

Since the recipe calls for only half a pineapple, chill the rest and serve it for breakfast.

Sautéed Pineapple Slices with Toasted Brioches and Ice Cream

1 fresh pineapple
5⅓ tablespoons sweet butter
4 to 8 tablespoons granulated sugar
2 to 3 tablespoons rum
2 stale brioches, cut in half, or 4 slices pound cake
Confectioners' sugar (optional)
1 pint coffee ice cream

1. Cut pineapple in half lengthwise. Cut 1 half in half again; reserve other half for another meal. Remove core from pineapple quarters and discard core. Slide thin-bladed serrated knife between flesh and shell, and lift out flesh. Cut it crosswise into ¾-inch slices.
2. Heat 4 tablespoons of the butter in skillet and gently cook pineapple slices, on both sides, several minutes on medium-high heat. Sprinkle with 2 to 4 tablespoons of the granulated sugar, depending on sweetness of pineapple, and cook until lightly caramelized.
3. Heat rum and pour over pineapple. Flame rum and cook 1 minute longer, shaking pan. Cool slightly.
4. Toast brioches until golden. Sprinkle 1 side with the remaining granulated sugar and broil until caramelized. Watch to see corners do not burn.
5. Place slice of brioche on each serving plate. Spoon pineapple over it and sprinkle with confectioners' sugar, if desired. Serve at once with scoops of ice cream.

Christopher Styler

MENU 1 (Right)
Sautéed Chicken Breasts
with Mustard and Gherkins
Rice Pilaf with Carrots, Celery, and Mushrooms

MENU 2
Poached Chicken Breasts
with Tomato Mayonnaise
Sauté of Two Squashes

MENU 3
Roasted Chicken Breasts
with New Potatoes and Shallots
Broccoli with Orange Sauce

Christopher Styler grew up cooking and never once doubted that his vocation was to be a professional cook. Now a developer of recipes for a restaurant consulting firm as well, he has devised three remarkable chicken dishes here: in Menu 1, a sauté of boneless chicken breasts with a creamy mustard sauce; in Menu 2, a cool summer dish garnished with fresh tomato mayonnaise; and in Menu 3, roast chicken breasts in pan gravy with shallots and potatoes. His approach to cooking is fourfold, and you need no professional training to practice the Styler philosophy. First, he advises, always use ingredients in season and cook them simply. Second, remember that sauces, spices, and herbs work best as accents, not disguises, and that meats and vegetables should always taste like what they are. Taste and taste again as you cook, and use a light hand when adding seasonings. You can easily add a little more mustard to the sauce in Menu 1, for example, or a little more pepper to the roast breasts in Menu 3, if you decide more is needed. But hiding a major overdose of spices or herbs is impossible. Third, you should cook to please yourself and your family and guests. Finally, think of a recipe as a helpful guide, not a book of laws, and if you personally like a dish with a touch more or less of anything—including cooking time—go ahead and try it that way.

A rich sauce—heavy cream and strong stock, with touches of brandy, leek, and mustard, and a garnish of chopped gherkins or sour pickles—turns chicken breasts into a satisfying meal, particularly with a rice pilaf on the side and a platter of fruit to go with after-dinner coffee.

Sautéed Chicken Breasts with Mustard and Gherkins
Rice Pilaf with Carrots, Celery, and Mushrooms

What makes this dish particularly memorable is the sauce. Cream based, it combines mustard with leeks (the mildest kind of onion) and tiny pickles, either dill gherkins or sour *cornichons*. Gherkins are the smallest of cucumbers, gathered green and crisp and then pickled in vinegar with various herbs and spices. You can find sweet or dill gherkins on the condiment shelf of any supermarket. *Cornichons* are the same size but pickled sour (with vinegar, small onions, chilies, and sometimes thyme or cloves). They are particularly tasty with homemade pâtés, and good French restaurants usually serve them that way. You may have to go to a specialty shop to find the real French sour *cornichons*, which are expensive but wonderfully distinct in flavor. Either pickle will do for this recipe, and dill gherkins are certainly easier to find.

Another essential element in the sauce is coarse mustard, which contains whole mustard seed and usually comes in a crock with a cork stopper. (*Moutarde de meaux* is the French name, and imported coarse mustard is often sold in the gourmet department in supermarkets and always in specialty shops.) The smoother Dijon mustard is more familiar for sauces and dressings; but coarse mustard is sweeter and more complex in flavor—and worth keeping on hand for sandwiches and cold meats, as well as for an occasional hearty sauce.

Leeks are a typical fall vegetable, though you can find them year round in most large markets, usually in bunches of three to five. They have a delicate savoriness very different from the flavor of an ordinary white onion. Choose the ones with the greenest tops and medium-size necks—the largest ones may be woody and flavorless. Wash leeks carefully: dirt gets caught in the oniony layers at the base.

CLEANING LEEKS

Fresh carrots and celery add a crunchy texture and good taste to the rice pilaf. Buy deep orange carrots. The deeper the orange, the sweeter the carrot and the more carotene (the source of vitamin A). Beware of carrots that look green or yellow at the top, as they will taste bitter. The best supermarket carrots come with their tops on, rather than prepackaged in plastic bags. But give the prepackaged kind a careful look over: if you avoid bruised or broken carrots, these can also be very good. If you do buy carrots with tops, be sure to cut the tops off before refrigerating them; the tops will draw out moisture in the refrigerator, and the carrots will wilt and turn limp. Store the carrots in a plastic bag. Carrot tops make an extra green for salad, if you like the flavor and appearance.

Pick out celery with no bruises or blemishes on the stalks, and look for crisp, leafy tops. White or blanched celery types are not as flavorful as the more familiar green variety, Pascal. To store, cut the stalks apart, wash, dry, and wrap in plastic.

Be careful not to overcook the vegetables for the pilaf. If you chop them as the recipe directs, into half-inch dices, they will be done in five minutes at the most.

WHAT TO DRINK

This main dish featuring mustard and *cornichons* in the sauce calls for a wine with more body than most whites have. Choose a good white Burgundy—a Meursault. Or switch colors and enjoy a young Beaujolais.

SHOPPING LIST AND STAPLES

4 skinless, boneless chicken breast halves
1 medium-size onion
1 stalk celery
1 carrot
2 medium-size leeks
8 large fresh mushrooms (about ¼ pound)
5 tablespoons butter
½ cup heavy cream
2½ cups chicken broth
2 tablespoons minced dill gherkins or *cornichons*
1 tablespoon coarse mustard
2 tablespoons peanut oil
1 cup long-grain white rice
½ cup flour
Salt and pepper

2 tablespoons Cognac or sherry

UTENSILS

Large skillet with cover
Medium-size heavy saucepan with cover
Baking sheet
Measuring cups and spoons
Chef's knife
Paring knife
Vegetable peeler
Tongs
Waxed paper

START-TO-FINISH STEPS

1. Follow chicken recipe steps 1 through 3.
2. Follow pilaf recipe steps 1 through 3. As rice and vegetables simmer, follow chicken recipe steps 4 through 8.
3. Serve chicken and rice pilaf.

RECIPES

Sautéed Chicken Breasts with Mustard and Gherkins

4 skinless, boneless chicken breast halves
Salt and freshly ground black pepper
½ cup flour for dredging
2 medium-size leeks
1 tablespooon butter
2 tablespoons peanut oil
2 tablespoons Cognac or sherry
1 cup chicken broth
½ cup heavy cream
2 tablespoons minced gherkins
1 tablespoon coarse mustard

1. Slice each chicken breast in half horizontally and flatten between 2 sheets of waxed paper.
2. Sprinkle chicken pieces lightly with salt and pepper.
3. Dredge in flour, shaking off excess. Set aside.
4. Trim off root ends of leeks and split them lengthwise. Rinse under cold running water, peeling back layers of leeks to remove all sand and grit (see diagram on the opposite page). Cut into ¼-inch dice.
5. Heat butter and oil in large skillet over medium heat until butter is foaming. Add as many chicken pieces as will fit comfortably in skillet at 1 time. Sauté 1 to 1½ minutes on each side until golden brown. Repeat with the remaining chicken. Add more butter if necessary. Place sautéed chicken on baking sheet and keep warm in 200-degree oven.
6. Using same skillet, sauté leeks on low heat until wilted, about 4 minutes. Add Cognac and boil until almost evaporated, about 1 minute. Add stock, scraping up brown bits that cling to pan, and simmer until stock is reduced by half—about 3 minutes.
7. Add cream, gherkins, mustard, and pepper. Simmer

until thick enough to lightly coat spoon, about 3 minutes.
8. Return chicken to pan, turning with tongs to coat with sauce. Cover and simmer until heated through, about 2 minutes. Overlap chicken pieces on warmed serving platter. Pour remaining sauce over.

Rice Pilaf with Carrots, Celery, and Mushrooms

1 medium-size onion
1 carrot, peeled
1 stalk celery
8 large fresh mushrooms (about ¼ pound)
4 tablespoons butter
1 cup long-grain white rice
2 cups chicken broth or water
½ teaspoon salt

1. Cut onion, carrot, and celery into ½-inch dice. Wipe mushrooms with dampened paper towels to remove dirt. Cut into ½-inch dice.
2. Melt butter in saucepan over medium heat. When foam subsides, add vegetables and sauté until softened—about 5 minutes—stirring occasionally.
3. Add rice, tossing to coat with butter. Add stock and salt. Reduce heat to very low. Cook, covered, until rice and vegetables are tender, about 20 minutes. Remove from heat and fluff with fork. Rice can be kept warm off heat up to 10 minutes.

ADDED TOUCH

If fresh raspberries are unavailable, blueberries or blackberries will do very well for this dessert. Or use frozen raspberries, but drain off the juice.

Raspberry and Peach Compote

1 large peach
½ cup sugar
½ cup water
1 teaspoon fresh lemon juice
½ cup champagne or white wine, or 2 tablespoons light rum
1-pint basket raspberries

1. Plunge peach into boiling water and boil until skin is loosened, about 1 minute. Remove with slotted spoon. Rinse under cold running water until cool enough to handle. Slip off skin.
2. Combine sugar, water, and lemon juice in small heavy saucepan. Heat over medium heat, stirring constantly, until sugar is dissolved and syrup is boiling, about 3 minutes. Add champagne and boil additional 2 minutes.
3. While syrup is boiling, cut peach in half and discard pit. Cut peach halves into ¼-inch slices. Arrange alternating slices of peach with raspberries in 1½-quart heat-proof bowl.
4. Pour syrup over fruit in bowl. Fit small plate over fruit. Place 1-pound weight, such as 1-cup measure filled ¾ full with water, over plate. Refrigerate until time to serve.

Poached Chicken Breasts with Tomato Mayonnaise
Sauté of Two Squashes

Ripe summer tomatoes flavor and color the mayonnaise dressing for these poached chicken breasts with summer squashes.

Mayonnaise is simply a combination of egg and oil, beaten together until they combine. With a blender or food processor, mayonnaise (which used to require a whisk and a lot of time) becomes one of the easiest sauces to make—the foundation of a dozen other sauces, such as this one with fresh tomatoes.

Use a soft spatula to aid in blending and be sure to turn the motor off as you stir, or to keep the spatula safely away from the blades. Taste the mayonnaise as you proceed and adjust the seasonings so that you achieve a light, subtle flavor. Only ripe tomatoes will do. Serve the meal, an ideal summer supper, at room temperature.

WHAT TO DRINK

A fruity white wine, served cold, is best for this meal. A Vouvray from the Loire valley or an Italian Pinot Grigio or Pinot Bianco would be perfect. A dry sparkling wine from New York or California would also be appropriate.

SHOPPING LIST AND STAPLES

2 whole skinless, boneless chicken breasts
3 medium-size tomatoes

1 bunch celery
2 medium-size zucchini
2 medium-size yellow squashes
2 scallions
1 bunch fresh parsley
2 tablespoons chopped fresh basil, or 2 teaspoons dried
1 lemon
3 tablespoons butter
1 egg
¾ cup peanut oil
¼ teaspoon dry mustard
¼ teaspoon Cayenne pepper
¾ teaspoon chopped fresh thyme, or ¼ teaspoon dried
Salt and pepper
¼ teaspoon white peppercorns
1 cup dry white wine (optional)

UTENSILS

Blender or food processor
Large skillet
Large saucepan
Small saucepan
Measuring cups and spoons
Chef's knife
All-purpose knife
Paring knife
Slotted spoon
Rubber spatula
Tongs
Instant-reading meat thermometer

START-TO-FINISH STEPS

1. Core tomato, juice lemon, and chop basil or parsley for tomato mayonnaise recipe. Chop scallions, tomatoes, and celery leaves for chicken recipe.
2. Follow chicken recipe steps 1 and 2.
3. Follow tomato mayonnaise recipe steps 1 through 5.
4. Follow squash recipe step 1.
5. Follow chicken recipe step 3.
6. Follow squash recipe steps 2 and 3.
7. Follow chicken recipe step 4, and serve with squashes.

RECIPES

Poached Chicken Breasts

2 quarts water
1 cup dry white wine (optional)
½ cup chopped celery leaves
10 sprigs fresh parsley
2 scallions, split lengthwise
1 teaspoon salt
¼ teaspoon white peppercorns
2 whole skinless, boneless chicken breasts
Tomato mayonnaise (see following recipe)
2 tomatoes, sliced
Parsley

1. Put water, wine, celery leaves, parsley, scallions, salt, and peppercorns in large saucepan. Bring to a boil.
2. Add chicken breasts. Adjust heat to maintain bare simmer. Poach until instant-reading meat thermometer inserted into thickest part of breast registers 180–185 degrees—about 20 minutes.
3. Remove with tongs and drain well on paper towels. Cool until chicken can be handled, about 2 to 3 minutes.
4. Slice chicken lengthwise into ¼-inch slices. Arrange, slightly overlapping, on large platter. Spread tomato mayonnaise over chicken. Serve at room temperature. Garnish with sliced tomatoes and parsley.

Tomato Mayonnaise

1 ripe tomato, cored
1 egg
1 teaspoon lemon juice
½ teaspoon salt
¼ teaspoon dry mustard
¼ teaspoon Cayenne pepper
¾ cup peanut oil
2 tablespoons chopped fresh basil or parsley,
    or 2 teaspoons dried basil

1. Bring small saucepan of water to a boil.
2. Plunge tomato into boiling water until skin loosens, about 15 seconds. Remove tomato with slotted spoon. Run under cold water until cool enough to handle; slip off skin.
3. Cut tomato in half crosswise and squeeze each half firmly to remove seeds. Place cut side down on paper towels to drain.
4. Place egg, lemon juice, salt, mustard, and Cayenne in container of blender or food processor. Blend on low speed until smooth. With motor running, add oil in slow, steady stream. Continue blending until all oil is incorporated.
5. Chop tomato, drain off juice, and add with basil to food processor. Blend on low speed, scraping sides of container with rubber spatula as necessary, until tomato is pureed and basil is finely chopped.

Sauté of Two Squashes

2 medium-size yellow squashes
2 medium-size zucchini
3 tablespoons butter
¾ teaspoon chopped fresh thyme, or ¼ teaspoon dried
½ teaspoon salt
⅛ teaspoon freshly ground black pepper

1. Wash squashes and zucchini under cold running water. Trim stem and blossom ends with paring knife. Cut into 2-inch lengths. Cut each piece lengthwise into ½-inch slices. Stack slices and cut into ½-inch julienne strips.
2. Heat butter until foamy, in large skillet over medium heat. Add squash and toss until coated with butter.
3. Sauté, tossing, until crisp but tender, about 4 minutes. Increase heat to high. Sprinkle with thyme, salt, and pepper. Cook, tossing, until squash is lightly browned, about 2 minutes.

Roasted Chicken Breasts with New Potatoes and Shallots
Broccoli with Orange Sauce

Serve the main dish on one large platter. The shallots will add a full aroma to the dish. Parsley is a nice decorative touch.

Roasting chicken breasts and new potatoes in their skins, seasoned only with shallots, salt, and pepper, produces a dish that looks as satisfying as it tastes. It also proves Christopher Styler's point that when dealing with fresh ingredients, simplicity is the best policy. The dinner is not only delicious but is unhurried to get ready. Once the main dish is in the oven, you need only prepare the broccoli and oranges and then make a simple sauce when the chicken is done.

While the chicken and vegetables roast together, their flavors and fragrances mingle, and a delicious juice forms in the bottom of the casserole—the basis for a good pan gravy. The recipe works equally well with chicken thighs and legs, but then choose slightly larger potatoes and increase the cooking time by 5 or 10 minutes. Do not use wings, since they would be done before the potatoes. Save the wings for the stockpot.

Nearly any green vegetable would make a good side dish, but nothing tastes better with this meal than the broccoli with orange segments and a tart orange sauce. Use a California navel orange, which peels easily and breaks into plump, attractive segments. Navel oranges are ripe from November through May only, so in other months substitute a Valencia orange.

Alsatian wines would combine well with this menu: a Gewürztraminer of fairly recent vintage or a more delicate Riesling, also young, would be ideal.

SHOPPING LIST AND STAPLES

4 unskinned boneless chicken breast halves
12 small new potatoes
1 bunch broccoli (about 1¼ pounds)
8 shallots
1 navel orange
5 tablespoons butter
1 cup chicken broth
1 tablespoon flour
Salt and pepper
1 bunch parsley (optional)

UTENSILS

Medium-size saucepan with cover
Large roasting pan
Colander
Measuring cups and spoons
All-purpose knife
Slotted spoon
Whisk

START-TO-FINISH STEPS

1. Follow chicken recipe steps 1 through 3.
2. Follow broccoli recipe steps 1 through 3.
3. Follow chicken recipe step 4.
4. Follow broccoli recipe steps 4 and 5.
5. Follow chicken recipe step 5, and serve with broccoli.

RECIPES

Roasted Chicken Breasts with New Potatoes and Shallots

3 tablespoons butter, softened
4 unskinned boneless chicken breast halves
12 small new potatoes
8 shallots
½ teaspoon salt
⅛ teaspoon freshly ground black pepper
1 tablespoon flour
1 cup chicken broth

1. Heat oven to 400 degrees.
2. Butter roasting pan large enough to hold chicken breasts in 1 layer. Spread skin side of breasts with the remaining butter. Place skin side up in pan.
3. Scrub potatoes and peel shallots. Cut both in half. Scatter around chicken and sprinkle all with salt and pepper. Cover pan with aluminum foil. Place in oven and

roast 15 minutes.
4. Uncover pan. Baste and continue roasting until potatoes are tender and chicken is golden, 20 to 30 minutes.
5. Transfer chicken, potatoes, and shallots to warmed serving platter. Cover platter and keep warm in turned-off oven with door slightly ajar.
6. Pour off all but 2 tablespoons of the drippings from pan. Place pan over medium-low heat and add flour. Cook, stirring with whisk, 3 minutes, or until mixture is golden. Add stock and continue cooking and stirring until sauce is smooth. Simmer over low heat 3 to 5 minutes and taste, adding salt and pepper if necessary.
7. Drizzle half of the sauce over chicken and potatoes and pass remaining sauce separately. Garnish platter with parsley sprigs, if desired.

Broccoli with Orange Sauce

½ teaspoon salt
1 bunch broccoli (about 1¼ pounds)
1 navel orange
2 tablespoons butter

1. Fill saucepan halfway with cold water. Add ¼ teaspoon of the salt. Bring to a boil, covered, over high heat.
2. Trim broccoli, leaving 3-inch stem. Cut lengthwise into spears, each containing some flowerets.
3. Cut orange in half. Cut between membranes of 1 half with knife to free segments. Cut segments crosswise into ½-inch pieces and reserve. Squeeze juice from the remaining half of orange and reserve 3 tablespoons.
4. Cook broccoli spears in boiling water, uncovered, until crisp but tender, about 5 minutes. Drain in colander and arrange on serving platter.
5. Melt butter in same saucepan over medium heat. Add the remaining ¼ teaspoon salt and reserved orange juice and segments. Remove from heat and spoon sauce over broccoli.

ADDED TOUCH

A dessert might be in order with this menu. If you want something more elaborate than a basket of fresh fruit, try the recipe below.

Broiled Persimmons with Bourbon Butter

2 medium-size persimmons
2 tablespoons bourbon or rum
2 tablespoons dark brown sugar
3 tablespoons melted butter

1. Split persimmons through stem end, leaving stem intact. Score cut side of persimmons ½ inch deep with paring knife in checkered pattern. Heat broiler.
2. Mix bourbon and brown sugar in small bowl, then stir in butter. Spoon over persimmon halves slowly, allowing it to soak in. Broil in broiler pan, 3 inches from heat, until sugar is bubbly and golden brown—about 3 minutes. Transfer to serving dishes, spooning juices left in pan over them.

Bert Greene

MENU 1 (Left)
Marinated Rock Cornish Game Hens
Baked Fennel with Parmesan Cheese
Green Herbed Rice

MENU 2
Chicken with Scallions
Steamed Rice
Herbed Tomatoes

MENU 3
Virginia Fried Chicken with Cream Gravy
Baked Spoon Bread
Green Beans with Sautéed Sweet Peppers

L ike most of America, I dine on poultry more than on any other meat these days—and without complaint, mind you," says author-cook Bert Greene. He recalls that as a child he often ate chicken or game hens, usually boiled and always overdone. These memories have prompted him as an adult to cook chicken with care and respect—and never to boil it.

In Menu 1, the game hens are baked. Because of the rich marinade for the hens and the side dish of fennel—a licorice-flavored celery that you can buy only in fall and winter—Menu 1 is an excellent cold-weather dinner. You should probably reserve sautéed and simmered chicken in Menu 2 for summer, since it requires fresh herbs and the ripest possible tomatoes. The technique for cooking rice in both these menus is an innovation of Bert Greene's. He boils the rice, then sets it to steam slowly, covering it with paper toweling. The slow steaming not only keeps the grains separate but is a foolproof method of keeping the rice hot for an hour or more.

For Menu 3, an any-season variation on the Southern classic of chicken with cream gravy, Bert Greene uses a technique he calls Virginia fry. The spoon bread, served on the side, is another Southern favorite; but the vegetable—green beans with sweet red peppers—is a typical California stir-fry dish.

All three menus reflect Bert Greene's admiration for the boundless variety in American cooking. "What I love best about it," he observes, "is how it changes according to the cook's geography. Regional American dishes are like the patterns of a patchwork quilt. They take on their true substance only when they are combined."

The aromas from this dinner as it comes to the table will appeal to your guests as much as will its elegant look. The game hens, split in half and broiled, carry the scent of ginger, coriander, soy sauce, and orange, while basil and scallions make the rice fragrant. The fennel has just a hint of melted Parmesan cheese.

Marinated Rock Cornish Game Hens
Baked Fennel with Parmesan Cheese
Green Herbed Rice

One advantage of this recipe for game hens is that it calls for a marinade, so you can do some preparation ahead. The morning before, or even the day before, you plan to serve this dinner, take about 15 minutes to split the game hens and make the marinade. Your total work time for the entire meal will be under an hour.

Marinades not only add flavor to meats but also tenderize them, and in this case the orange peel—because of the citric acid—does both. Peel the orange with a knife, not with your fingers, and be sure to include the white pith along with the peel. Save the marinade at each step: the game hens bake in it; and then it forms the basis for the sauce, to which you add (among other good things) crushed red pepper. Brands of red pepper flakes vary considerably in fieriness. The hottest kind comes from Thailand; you will find it in Oriental markets. But if Thai pepper is unavailable, Korean or Indonesian will do.

Fennel—or anise—looks somewhat like celery but has a large bulb at the base. Flat, elongated bulbs are the best kind for cooking. Choose firm, crisp bulbs, not more than four inches wide, and pale, greenish white in color.

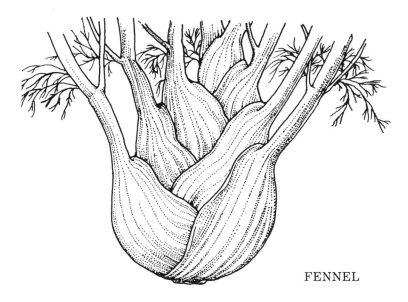

FENNEL

WHAT TO DRINK

Though you may automatically think of white wine when serving chicken, this company dinner would go very well with a red wine—Bert Greene suggests an imported Bordeaux. Alternatively, you might certainly serve a white wine, for example a California Riesling.

SHOPPING LIST AND STAPLES

4 small Rock Cornish game hens
1 bunch scallions
3 large fennel bulbs
1 bunch fresh parsley
3 tablespoons fresh chopped basil, or 1 tablespoon dried
3 cloves garlic
1 branch ginger root
1 orange
¼ pound Parmesan cheese
3½ tablespoons butter
1 cup plus 1 tablespoon soy sauce
½ cup olive oil
1 tablespoon sesame oil
1 teaspoon vinegar
⅔ cup long-grain white rice
1½ tablespoons brown sugar
2 tablespoons honey
½ teaspoon ground coriander
1 small bay leaf
¼ teaspoon crushed red pepper
Salt and pepper

UTENSILS

Blender or food processor
2 large saucepans
Small saucepan
2 shallow baking pans
Medium-size baking dish
Colander to fit in large saucepan
Strainer
Measuring cups and spoons
Chef's knife or poultry shears
All-purpose knife
Grater
Zester
Bulb baster
Pastry brush

START-TO-FINISH STEPS

In the morning: follow game hen recipe step 1.

1. Chop ginger root and peel orange for game hen marinade. Mince garlic, ginger root, and scallions for game hen sauce. Grate Parmesan cheese for fennel recipe, grating extra for rice recipe, if desired. Chop basil and scallion

tops for rice recipe.

2. Follow game hen recipe steps 2 and 3. While game hens roast, follow rice recipe steps 1 and 2. As rice simmers, follow fennel recipe step 1.

3. Follow game hen recipe steps 4 and 5.

4. Follow fennel recipe steps 2 through 5.

5. Follow rice recipe steps 3 and 4.

6. Follow game hen recipe step 6, and serve with rice and fennel.

RECIPES

Marinated Rock Cornish Game Hens

The game hens:
4 small Rock Cornish game hens, split down breast and flattened

The marinade:
1 cup soy sauce
Peel of 1 orange
½ teaspoon chopped ginger root
2 cloves garlic
½ teaspoon ground coriander
Freshly ground black pepper
1 small bay leaf
2 tablespoons honey

The sauce:
2 teaspoons olive oil
1 teaspoon minced garlic
1 teaspoon minced ginger root
1 tablespoon minced scallions
¼ teaspoon crushed red pepper
1 tablespoon soy sauce
1 teaspoon vinegar
1½ tablespoons brown sugar
1 tablespoon water
1 tablespoon sesame oil

1. In the morning, flatten game hens and combine marinade ingredients in blender or food processor. Blend until smooth. Place hens, skin side down, on 2 baking pans and pour marinade over them. Refrigerate and remove 1 hour before preparation.

2. Preheat oven to 450 degrees.

3. Place baking sheets with hens in oven and bake 35 to 40 minutes. Baste often with marinade, using bulb baster.

4. To make sauce, heat olive oil in small saucepan over medium-low heat. Stir in minced garlic, ginger root, and scallions; add crushed red pepper. Cook 2 minutes. Add soy sauce, vinegar, brown sugar, and water. Cook, stirring, 1 minute.

5. Strain sauce and add sesame oil. Sauce will thicken as it sits.

6. Just before serving, use pastry brush to coat hens with sauce

Baked Fennel with Parmesan Cheese

3 large fennel bulbs
Salt and freshly ground black pepper

¼ cup freshly grated Parmesan cheese
2½ tablespoons butter

1. Bring salted water to a boil in large saucepan.

2. Cut away any wilted or bruised parts of fennel (see drawing on the opposite page). Cut off and discard tops and trim bottoms. Cut fennel in half, place cut side down, and slice lengthwise into ¼-inch slices. Place in boiling water to cover, and cook about 6 minutes, or until almost tender. Drain under cold running water until cool. Drain again and pat dry.

3. Layer half of the fennel slices over bottom of lightly buttered baking dish. Sprinkle with salt, pepper, and half of the grated cheese. Dot with half of the butter.

4. Layer on the remaining fennel slices. Sprinkle with salt, pepper, and the remaining cheese. Dot with the remaining butter.

5. Bake in 450-degree oven until top is lightly golden, about 15 minutes.

Green Herbed Rice

4 quarts lightly salted water
⅔ cup long-grain white rice
½ cup fresh parsley
3 tablespoons fresh chopped basil, or 1 tablespoon dried
1½ tablespoons chopped scallion tops
¼ to ½ cup olive oil
Salt and freshly ground black pepper
1 tablespoon butter
Freshly grated Parmesan cheese (optional)

1. Bring 4 quarts of lightly salted water to a boil in large saucepan. Add rice to boiling water. Stir once so that rice does not stick to bottom of pan. Reheat to boiling. Reduce heat and simmer until just tender, about 12 minutes. Drain in colander. Do not rinse.

2. Put 2 inches of water into same saucepan and put colander with rice into pan. Do not let water touch colander. Heat water to boiling. Cover rice with 1 layer of paper towels. Steam at least 15 minutes. (Rice can be steamed for as long as an hour without damage, but add more water to saucepan as necessary.)

3. Place parsley, basil, and scallion tops in blender or food processor container. Slowly add just enough olive oil to make smooth puree.

4. Just before serving, toss rice with herb puree until well mixed and green in color. Add salt and pepper to taste. Stir in butter and sprinkle with Parmesan cheese, if desired.

LEFTOVER SUGGESTION

Cold game hen comes in handy for next day's lunch, so you may want to broil an extra bird for planned leftovers. Combine the cold meat with slivers of Belgian endive and cherry tomatoes, and toss with a tart, lemony dressing: half olive oil, half lemon juice, and salt to taste.

Chicken with Scallions
Steamed Rice
Herbed Tomatoes

Tomatoes at their peak, together with firm plump scallions, are essential to this menu; midsummer is the best time to find both. Fresh basil and oregano (dried will do in a pinch), will also improve the stuffed tomatoes.

The chicken recipe also calls for bruised garlic—a good technique for any cook to know. To bruise a garlic clove, press it on a flat surface with the blade of a knife, pushing just hard enough to release some of the juices. The peel will virtually pop off. This produces a different flavor from chopping and mincing garlic or cooking it whole in its skin. The smaller you chop the pieces of a garlic clove, the more powerful their flavor becomes. Cooking garlic whole adds a very mild flavor. A bruised clove is stronger than a whole one but not as strong as a minced one.

When you shop, you may want to get a loaf of very good French or Italian bread. The velvety sauce for the chicken and scallions is too good to leave on the plate, and a piece of crusty bread will absorb it deliciously.

WHAT TO DRINK

The cream sauce here is rich, so choose a full-bodied white wine, preferably a California Chardonnay or a Burgundy.

SHOPPING LIST AND STAPLES

4-pound chicken, cut into serving pieces
2 or 3 bunches scallions (about 18)
4 medium-size ripe tomatoes
3 shallots
1 bunch fresh parsley
1 clove garlic
1 tablespoon minced fresh basil, or 1 teaspoon dried
1 tablespoon minced fresh oregano, or 1 teaspoon dried
½ cup heavy cream
4 tablespoons butter
1 egg
1½ cups chicken broth
6 tablespoons dry unflavored bread crumbs
1 tablespoon vegetable oil
3 tablespoons olive oil
½ cup flour
1⅓ cups long-grain white rice
⅛ teaspoon ground allspice
Pinch of ground cloves
Salt and pepper
¼ cup dry white wine

Bring the chicken, scallions, and sauce to the table on the same platter with the steamed rice and herbed tomatoes. As you serve, spoon the sauce over the chicken and rice—but not the tomatoes, which are best plain.

UTENSILS

Dutch oven or casserole with cover
Large heavy skillet
Large saucepan
Flameproof baking dish
1 medium-size bowl
2 small bowls
Colander to fit inside large saucepan
Strainer
Measuring cups and spoons
Chef's knife
Tongs
Whisk

START-TO-FINISH STEPS

1. Bruise garlic and follow chicken recipe steps 1 and 2.
2. Put water on to boil for rice recipe.
3. Chop herbs for tomatoes and follow tomato recipe steps 1 and 2.
4. Chop parsley and scallions, then follow chicken recipe steps 3 and 4.
5. Follow rice recipe step 1. As rice simmers, follow tomato recipe step 3.
6. Follow rice recipe step 2.
7. Follow chicken recipe step 5.
8. Follow tomato recipe step 4. As tomatoes bake and broil, follow chicken recipe step 6.
9. Serve tomatoes and rice with chicken.

RECIPES

Chicken with Scallions

4-pound chicken, cut into serving pieces
1 clove garlic, bruised
½ cup flour
½ teaspoon salt
Freshly ground black pepper
⅛ teaspoon ground allspice
4 tablespoons butter
1 tablespoon vegetable oil
¼ cup chopped scallions
¼ cup dry white wine
1½ cups chicken broth
16 scallions, trimmed, with 1½-inch green stems
1 egg yolk
½ cup heavy cream
Pinch of ground cloves
¼ cup chopped parsley

1. Rub chicken pieces well with bruised garlic. Discard garlic. Combine flour, salt, pepper, and allspice in paper bag. Add chicken, several pieces at a time. Shake well to coat; reserve excess flour.
2. Heat 3 tablespoons of the butter with oil in skillet over medium heat. Sauté chicken pieces about 10 minutes, or until deep golden brown on all sides. Transfer to Dutch oven or casserole.

3. Remove all but 1 tablespoon of the fat from skillet. Add the remaining tablespoon of butter and chopped scallions. Cook over medium-low heat 2 minutes. Stir in 2 tablespoons of the reserved flour mixture and cook over low heat, stirring constantly, 2 minutes. Whisk in wine and chicken broth. Heat to boiling and pour over chicken.
4. Reheat chicken until liquid boils. Reduce heat and cook, covered, over medium-low heat 20 minutes. Add whole scallions, only white bulbs covered by stock. Cook, covered, 5 minutes, or until chicken is tender. The scallions should still be slightly crunchy. Transfer chicken and scallions to shallow serving dish. Cover and keep warm.
5. Strain sauce into medium-size bowl, return it to skillet, and heat it to boiling. Boil until slightly thickened, about 5 minutes. Remove from heat.
6. Combine egg yolk with cream in small bowl. Add pinch of ground cloves. Stir into sauce. Return sauce to medium-low heat and cook 2 minutes. Do not boil or sauce will curdle. Season to taste and pour over chicken. Sprinkle with chopped parsley.

Steamed Rice

4 quarts salted water
1⅓ cups long-grain white rice

1. In saucepan, bring 4 quarts of salted water to a boil. Add rice, stirring so that it does not stick to bottom of pot. Reheat to boiling, then reduce heat to low. Simmer 12 to 15 minutes, or until just tender. Drain in colander, but do not rinse.
2. Using same pot in which rice was cooked, place colander with rice over 2 inches of water. Do not let water touch colander. Heat water to boiling. Cover rice with one layer of paper towels and steam at least 15 minutes.

Herbed Tomatoes

4 medium-size ripe tomatoes
Salt
6 tablespoons fine bread crumbs
2 tablespoons minced shallots
3 tablespoons olive oil
1 small clove garlic, minced
1 tablespoon minced fresh parsley
1 tablespoon minced fresh basil, or 1 teaspoon dried
1 tablespoon minced fresh oregano, or 1 teaspoon dried
Freshly ground black pepper

1. Preheat oven to 400 degrees.
2. Cut tops off tomatoes. Scoop out juice and seeds with spoon; discard. Sprinkle each tomato lightly with salt. Turn upside down on paper towels and let stand 10 minutes.
3. Combine all the remaining ingredients except pepper in small bowl. Spoon mixture into tomatoes. Sprinkle with freshly ground black pepper.
4. Place tomatoes in baking dish. Bake 10 minutes. Turn oven to broil. Run tomatoes under flame to lightly brown tops.

Virginia Fried Chicken with Cream Gravy
Baked Spoon Bread
Green Beans with Sautéed Sweet Peppers

If you have a bright, checked tablecloth, this is the meal to use it with; straw mats would also go with this dinner. The spoon *bread—a cornmeal pudding that you serve with a spoon— comes to the table in its own casserole.*

This menu comes from Virginia, according to Bert Greene, but with some modifications on the familiar Southern recipe for fried chicken. Instead of deep frying in lard, first sauté the chicken in a mixture of butter and oil, then put it in the oven to bake for 20 to 25 minutes. And for fragrance and bite, the cream gravy gets a last-minute teaspoon of bourbon.

Spoon bread is an old-time dish that practiced cooks used to claim they just "threw together." Making perfect spoon bread is not difficult, but you should pay special attention to the eggs, which must be at room temperature. Separate them, breaking the shell as cleanly as you can, and passing the yolk back and forth until it comes loose from the white. Even a speck of yolk will keep the whites from beating stiff—the oil in the yolk weights them down. They stiffen as you beat air into them; though you can use a rotary beater or electric mixer, a whisk is really the best tool for the job. A copper bowl, as specified in the recipe, cuts down the whisking time. (The copper reacts electrostatically with the whites, making them rise.) A stainless-steel bowl works almost as well. In either case, the bowl must be perfectly clean. Avoid plastic, glass, or earthenware because the beating will take much longer.

WHAT TO DRINK

This classic American menu could be accompanied by any of several medium-bodied white wines. Try a Californian Sauvignon Blanc, a French Graves from a small chateau, or a Macon from the Burgundy area.

SHOPPING LIST AND STAPLES

4-pound chicken, cut into serving pieces
1 pound fresh green beans
2 large shallots
1 sweet red pepper
1 bunch fresh parsley
17 tablespoons butter (2 sticks plus 1 tablespoon)
1 cup heavy cream
2⅓ cups light cream or half-and-half
4 eggs
1 cup plus 3 tablespoons chicken broth
1 tablespoon honey
2 tablespoons vegetable oil
1 cup white cornmeal
1 teaspoon baking powder

Pinch of ground allspice
Whole nutmeg
1 tablespoon sugar
½ cup plus 2 tablespoons flour
Pinch of white pepper
Salt and pepper
1 teaspoon bourbon

UTENSILS

2 large heavy skillets
Large saucepan with cover
Medium-size saucepan
Large shallow baking dish
2-quart casserole or soufflé dish
Large copper bowl
Large bowl
Colander
Measuring cups and spoons
All-purpose knife
Nutmeg grater
Tongs
Whisk

START-TO-FINISH STEPS

1. Grate nutmeg and follow chicken recipe steps 1 through 4.
2. Follow spoon bread recipe steps 1 through 4.
3. Cut beans, red pepper, shallots, and parsley for green beans. Follow bean recipe step 1.
4. Follow chicken recipe step 5.
5. Follow bean recipe steps 2 and 3.
6. Follow chicken recipe step 6, and serve with spoon bread and beans.

RECIPES

Virginia Fried Chicken with Cream Gravy

4-pound chicken, cut into serving pieces
½ teaspoon salt
¼ teaspoon freshly ground black pepper
Pinch of ground allspice
⅛ teaspoon freshly grated nutmeg
½ cup plus 2 tablespoons flour
8 to 12 tablespoons butter (1 to 1½ sticks)
1 to 2 tablespoons vegetable oil
1 cup chicken broth
1 cup heavy cream

1 teaspoon bourbon
Parsley sprigs for garnish (optional)

1. Remove and discard skin from chicken pieces by grasping skin with paper towel and pulling hard.
2. Combine salt, pepper, allspice, nutmeg, and ½ cup of the flour in paper bag. Place chicken, a few pieces at a time, in bag and shake to coat evenly with flour mixture.
3. Melt 8 tablespoons of the butter with 1 tablespoon oil in skillet over medium-low heat. Do not let butter burn. When butter stops foaming, gently place chicken in skillet. Sauté until golden brown, about 10 minutes on each side. Add the remaining butter and more oil if needed. Using tongs, remove chicken and drain on paper towels.
4. Place chicken in baking dish and bake uncovered 20 to 25 minutes at 375 degrees.
5. Meanwhile, drain all but 2 tablespoons of the fat from skillet. Stir in the remaining 2 tablespoons of flour over low heat; cook, stirring constantly, 2 minutes. Whisk in chicken broth, scraping bottom and sides of pan. Stir in cream and continue cooking 15 minutes. Season to taste with salt and pepper.
6. Stir in bourbon. Spoon some gravy over chicken and serve the remaining gravy separately. Garnish chicken with parsley sprigs, if desired.

Baked Spoon Bread

2⅓ cups light cream or half-and-half
4 tablespoons butter
1 tablespoon sugar
1 tablespoon honey
½ teaspoon salt
1 cup white cornmeal
4 eggs, separated
1 teaspoon baking powder
Pinch of white pepper

1. Preheat oven to 375 degrees.
2. Combine cream, butter, sugar, honey, and salt in medium-size saucepan over low heat. Cook just until butter melts. Slowly add cornmeal, stirring constantly over low heat until mixture thickens. Do not boil.
3. Transfer cornmeal mixture to large bowl. Beat in egg yolks, one at a time, beating well after each addition. Add baking powder and white pepper.
4. Using large whisk, beat egg whites in copper bowl until stiff. Fold into cornmeal mixture. Pour into buttered cas-

serole or soufflé dish. Bake about 35 minutes, or until puffed and golden.

Green Beans with Sautéed Sweet Peppers

2½ cups water
1 pound fresh green beans, ends trimmed
2 large shallots, minced
1 tablespoon butter
1 sweet red pepper, cut into ¼-inch strips
3 tablespoons chicken broth
¼ cup chopped fresh parsley
Salt and freshly ground black pepper

1. Bring 2½ cups of water to a boil in large covered saucepan.
2. When water is boiling, add green beans and cook 1 minute. Pour immediately into colander and drain under cold running water.
3. In skillet over medium-low heat, sauté shallots in butter until golden. Stir in red pepper strips and cook 2 minutes. Stir in chicken broth; cook until peppers are tender but still crunchy, about 5 minutes. Add beans and cook until they are warmed through and most of liquid has evaporated. Add parsley and salt and pepper to taste.

ADDED TOUCH

If you have an ice cream freezer, try this special dessert.

Blueberry Blizzard

1 pint fresh blueberries, or 9-ounce package frozen unsweetened blueberries, defrosted
1 package (10 ounces) frozen raspberries, defrosted
1 cup sugar, preferably superfine
1 cup water
2 to 3 tablespoons orange liqueur, such as Triple Sec
1 cup heavy cream

1. Combine blueberries, raspberries with syrup, sugar, water, and orange liqueur in large bowl. Mix well.
2. Puree blueberry mixture in food processor (or in batches in blender) until smooth. Strain through sieve back into bowl.
3. Beat cream until soft peaks form. Fold into blueberry mixture.
4. Pour into canister of ice cream freezer and proceed according to manufacturer's instructions.
5. Place ice cream in freezer for at least ½ hour to set.

Acknowledgments

The Editors particularly wish to thank the following for their contributions to the conception and production of these books: Ezra Bowen; Judith Brennan; Elizabeth Schneider Colchie; Marion Flynn; Frieda Henry; Pearl Lau; Elizabeth Noll; Ann Topper; Jack Ubaldi.

The Editors would also like to thank the following for their courtesy in lending items for photography: Arabia of Finland; Baccarat, Inc.; Bazar Français; Brunschwig and Fils; Company; Charles F. Lamalle; China Seas® Home Port T.M.; Christofle Silver, Inc.; Colony; Commercial Aluminum Cookware Company; Conran's; Country Floors, Inc.; Creuset; D. Porthault, Inc.; Dansk International Designs, Ltd.; Dean and DeLuca; Design Concept Laminates by Formica Corp.; Ercuis; Fabindia; Fabrications; Farberware Subsidiary of Kidde; Fitz and Floyd; Cecily Fortescue; General Housewares; Georg Jensen Silversmiths; Georges Briard, Inc.; Ginori Fifth Avenue; Haviland Limoges; Hummelwerk; International China Company, Inc.; Jacques Jugeat; Jane Products, Inc.; J. G. Durand International; Kitchen Aid; Kosta Boda; The Lauffer Company; Laura Ashley; Leacock and Company; New Country Gear Year III by Hartstone; Oneida Silversmiths; Orrefors, Inc.; The Pfaltzgraff Company; Pottery Barn; Reed and Barton Silversmiths; Royal Copenhagen Porcelain; Staffordshire Potteries USA, Inc.; Supreme Cutlery; Wallace Silversmiths; Turpan and Sanders; Wedgwood; White-Westinghouse; Williams-Sonoma.

Illustrations by Ray Skibinski.

Index

Time-Life Books Inc. offers a wide range of fine recordings, including a Big Band series. For subscription information, call 1-800-621-7026, or write TIME-LIFE MUSIC, Time & Life Building, Chicago, Illinois 60611.

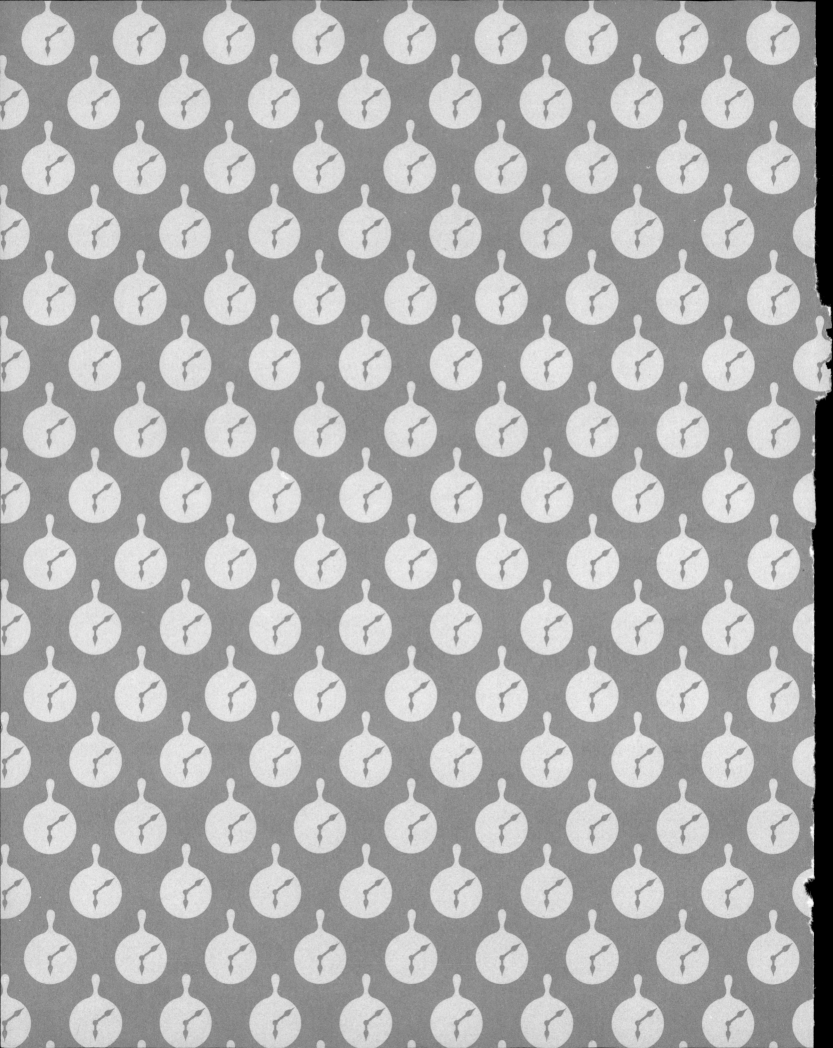